# The Golden Mean

# The Golden Mean
## Fostering young people's resilience, confidence and well-being

Morag Kerr (Editor)

# C|C|W|B press

First published by CCWB Press in 2018
Centre for Confidence and Well-being.
Registered Office: Abercorn House,
79 Renfrew Rd, Paisley, PA3 4DA
Registered charity number sco37080

**A catalogue record of this book is available
from the British Library**
978-0-9933527-8-2

Printed and bound in Great Britain by
Bell & Bain Ltd, Glasgow

POSTCARDS FROM SCOTLAND

Series editor: Carol Craig

Advisory group:
Professor Phil Hanlon, Chair,
Centre for Confidence and Well-being;
Fred Shedden

# Contents

# Foreword

A TRUTH that has to be faced is that for the infant entering the world that is modern day Scotland, life is challenging beyond all reason. Parenting, health, inequality, housing, education and stable and fair employment, all leave much to be desired. Opportunites to flourish? It's a case for too many that mere survival will have to do.

Some, but not all, of the reasons for this are down to decades of the dominance of free market ideas in politics and the running of the economy in the interests of the few. Some of it is therefore to do with the dysfunction in what we still consider our democracy. Other reasons arise from our culture in Scotland and what we have inherited by way of values and beliefs from previous generations.

And another hard truth. When I worked in the 1970s and 80s as a young teacher of troubled children and as a youth worker with marginalised and homeless teenagers, things were bad enough. More austerity and the galloping drink and drugs habit in all sections of society in recent decades make it so much worse for young people. Adverse Childhood Experiences for many of Scotland's young people must have increased with all the long term consequences for them and for the wider society.

As a young campaigner, I would not have been comfortable with the concept of the golden mean. Like many Scottish men and women who come out of marginal conditions and culture, I was too angry, indignant and impatient to consider such an apparently compliant notion. I could have been persuaded and I am now. For circumstances are so grotesquely skewed against so many children's and young people's life chances, that we are crying out for moderating influences.

No need to pretend the solutions are simple and straight-forward. But, as the following pages demonstrate convincingly, very often movingly, solutions there are. With a will, hope can prevail. In the outstanding initiatives written up in the challenging, informative and deeply thoughtful pages of this book, good things happen. This is an immensely hopeful book and it is good that in Scotland people write our stories in all their evident humanity and that the voices of young people themselves take centre stage.

Sure, there is a theme through many of these contributions that success is achieved almost in spite of the system and in the face of received wisdoms. The discussion, for example, on finding the balance between a caring support of the young and a challenging approach to stretch them on to high achievements is lost on many parents, teachers, policy makers and yes, politicians. They would do well to read and digest the thoughts and truly inspiring, touching and life-affirming practices and experiences they can encounter in the following pages.

No matter our material conditions, as individuals we can't make a sustaining life on our own. We are social beings and all sense of attainment, health and well-being flows from connectedness to others and membership of thriving and supportive communities.

Derek Rodger

# Introduction

Morag Kerr has taught in primary and secondary schools and in further education. Between 2005 and 2010 she was the Lead Specialist in Learning and Teaching for the Scottish Further Education Unit and is now the Support for Learning tutor at Newbattle Abbey College. For the past decade she has also worked extensively as a trainer/consultant in colleges and schools.

THE CENTRE for Confidence and Well-being publishes the Postcards from Scotland series. I have been involved in some way with the Centre since its official launch at the Scottish Parliament in 2005. I was then a frequent participant at the various events organised by the Centre. These were stimulating and brought together diverse groups of people and it felt exciting to be part of a movement which was challenging the way we lived our lives and seeking to find alternatives. In recent years I have been engaged by the Centre to provide training for schools on the *Bounce Back!* resilience programme.

When Carol Craig asked if I would be interested in editing a book about resilience my first thought was, 'That would be such a challenge, but what an interesting one.' I've spent my whole life in education. In my various roles I've always been fascinated by the learning process and how people, old and young, deal with it. Learning is not easy; it's often messy, challenging, frustrating and at times downright difficult. To be a successful learner you need to be resilient. Many children and young people find the challenge of learning daunting especially if they lack confidence and the resilience to stick at it when they feel they're not getting anywhere. I chose to work with learners who were 'reluctant' and challenging. I found that, while they often coped with very difficult home lives, they could not demonstrate the same resilience in learning that they showed outside school or college. And that is when I really became aware that the kind of support offered to young people can be the key to building their resilience and confidence.

When I looked for authors to contribute to the book I was particularly keen to find people or organisations offering exceptional ways to support the development of children and young people's confidence and resilience. As you read their chapters you will understand why I was keen for them to contribute.

The title for this Postcards book conveys the challenge adults face in providing the right level of support to young people: support that does not eliminate the courage to take risks. The concept of the Golden Mean comes from Greek philosophy and was particularly elaborated by Aristotle. He described it as 'the golden middle way' – the desirable mid point between two extremes, one of excess and the other of deficiency. For example, in the Aristotelian view, courage is a virtue, but if it's taken to excess it would manifest as recklessness. At the other extreme, it is cowardice.

What does this have to do with confidence and resilience? The various chapters in this book provide you with some excellent and insightful examples of why finding the balance, or middle way, between support and challenge is vital to developing young people's resilience, confidence and well-being.

In line with the aim of the Postcards from Scotland series this book is concerned with stimulating new thinking. The first two chapters of the book by Alan McLean and Carol Craig set out new ways to think about how best to develop children and young people.

In Scotland we have moved from the strict, authoritarian attitudes towards children which prevailed in the 1950s and 60s to one which tends to be soft, warm and potentially indulgent. This move is certainly an improvement on what went before but McLean and Craig both voice concerns that for some children the pendulum has swung too far in the other direction. Carol Craig in particular articulates the view that nowadays parents often over-protect their children. This means that young people are not allowed to experience the challenges that can help them to develop resilience. The long-term effect on their well-being is that, as adults, they may lack the strength to cope with the adversities that life inevitably delivers. Alan McLean explains the need for balance between support and challenge and gives us a language and a model to help us find that balance. Carol Craig explores the impact of different parenting styles on the health and well-being of children.

All the other authors have had first hand experience of working with young people to help them flourish, develop confidence and become resilient. There is a wealth of stories in this book. Stories which demonstrate ways young people can be supported to face adversities and challenges and find ways to overcome them. The stories span education, the arts, outdoor learning and the voluntary sector.

The authors are all passionate about the projects or initiatives they are, or have been, involved with. Many of the descriptions of the young people they have met are moving. The voices of the young people themselves are powerful, especially when describing the challenges they faced and how they overcame them. The key factor for all of them is the support they received and the belief that others had in them. This was particularly important when they were at the lowest, or most challenging, time of their lives.

Some of the stories are of young people experiencing severe hardship. Others are of young people being set challenges that take them out of their comfort zone but with the right level of support ultimately finding the resources within themselves to move forward and find solutions. The young people quoted here describe how their confidence grew and how hope is a major factor in keeping going when life is really tough. It is inspiring to read about how those working with young people can simultaneously let them know how much they are cherished and respected while also ensuring that they don't transgress important boundaries.

There are other learning points in this book. For example: experiencing play in the outdoors for young children is a key factor in flourishing; music can play a part in social transformation; an art room can become an 'incubator of courage'; learning in the outdoors can improve young people's mental well-being; and introducing school staff to activities that take them out of their comfort zone helps them identify their key strengths.

I am delighted that the journey I've been on with the Centre has led to the publication of this book. As readers will see this is not an academic book but rather a handbook for practitioners, parents, carers and anyone who is looking for ways to support young people to develop their resilience, confidence and well-being.

Morag Kerr, August 2018

# Building Resilience through Support and Challenge – the Golden Mean in Action

Alan McLean

A former Principal Education Psychologist, Alan McLean is the author of three books about motivation, the latest, *Knowing and Growing,* also a *Postcards from Scotland* publication. Alan has extensively researched what motivates learners and created a comprehensive framework to illustrate our needs and how they should be met for us to thrive, particularly the need for balance between support and challenge which provides the golden mean. His introductory chapter sets the context for the following sections of the book by giving a very accessible explanation of the need for challenge to be part of our development in order for us to become resilient.

THERE has been steady improvement in the quality of adult/ youth relations over recent decades and a shift away from coercive authority. Through the1980s and 1990s teaching was transformed from a punitive to a reward-based model, a shift from cold control to warm control. Through more recent initiatives such as Restorative Practice and Unicef's Rights Respecting School, the shift has been from a *control* to a *collaborative* culture.

We are now gradually moving beyond the rewards culture towards the vision outlined by the American philosopher and educator John Dewey more than a hundred years ago. Dewey believed that the inclination to learn is an intrinsic part of our nature but that it needs to be nurtured. Only fifty years ago the mantra in Scottish schools was 'Children should be seen and not heard'. Now we encourage young people to express themselves and the relationship has changed from one based on compliance to a more nuanced partnership. Authority is now about structure and influence and less about dominance and control. However, it is also vitally important that the pendulum doesn't swing too far to the other side. There is a middle ground or, in Aristotle's terminology, 'a golden mean'.

Recent initiatives driven by insights from attachment theory, nurture work and Adverse Childhood Experiences rightly aim to support disadvantaged young people. However, the empathic impulses driving these approaches put them at risk of over-protecting young people and thereby undermining their resilience. Support is vital but when we try to help too much we can unwittingly create dependency. We can also empathise too much and our attempts to understand some young people can become intrusive. While many will welcome professionals' interest in what has happened to them some may resent what they see as adults prying into their personal lives. Some may also *take liberties* in an attempt to provoke the controlling response they are used to.

This chapter introduces a model and a language to help us develop young people's resilience in a balanced way.

**The Ring model**

Our motives have evolved to meet our psychological needs. The more satisfied our needs, the more congruent and coherent our well-being. The table opposite pairs each of our underlying needs with its motive.

| Psychological need | Motive |
|---|---|
| Affiliation, a sense of belonging | To seek acceptance |
| Shared autonomy, a sense of collective power | To contribute to a common purpose |
| Agency, a sense of confidence | To make progress |
| Personal autonomy, a sense of individual power | To seek status |

We all have the same psychological needs but we overcome our challenges in our own unique way. For each individual some motives are stronger than others. Indeed these core preferences form the basis of the model presented here.

The conundrum at the heart of human relationships is that we have to balance our own needs with the needs of others. At the core of this tension lies *autonomy*. If you look at the psychological needs in the table above you will see that there are two types of autonomy, namely personal autonomy and shared autonomy. We are all driven by both to a greater or lesser extent.

■ Personal autonomy is 'making our mark' and achieving status. This is the preference to advance ourselves relative to, and in competition with, others. Personal autonomy is our need to determine our own goals and assert ourselves. It drives us to challenge ourselves.

■ Shared autonomy is 'being part of things', by contributing to a shared purpose. This is the

preference for aligning our goals and choices with
those of the group. Shared autonomy is our need to
collectively determine our aspirations. It drives us to
cooperate with others.

Most of us will have a preference for one of the two strands
of autonomy and this is central to understanding ourselves as
these are our key 'feel good' preferences.

Each strand of autonomy has its own foundational need.
Shared autonomy grows naturally out of the need for affiliation,
our need for belonging. Personal autonomy grows naturally out
of our need to exercise agency, our sense of feeling capable
and making progress.

Most of us have an intuitive understanding that qualities work
best when balanced, as in the phrase 'everything in moderation'.
No qualities are an unmitigated good – they can all be taken
too far or not far enough. As I have already suggested, the
intention to be helpful, when taken to excess, becomes intrusive.
But when it is deficient it becomes negligent. Aristotle's notion
of the golden mean shows that any desirable quality is the mid-
point between two extremes – a balance between too much
and too little. For example, courage is good, but if taken too far
it becomes recklessness. If it is diminished cowardice results.

The golden mean also implies that most virtues are a mix of
two interdependent qualities that shouldn't be considered
separately. To achieve moderation each quality requires to be
paired with a counterbalancing quality. For example, kindness
moderates the harshness and potentially devastating impact of
honesty when giving someone critical feedback.

To help visualise this dynamic I have created a Ring of
Preferences (Figure 1). The interlocking spirals have a bearing

on one another. The upper half of the Ring shows the spirals in balance, where the preferences are of similar weight. In the upper half the effect on our well-being is uplifting, below it spirals downwards into what I call the dark side. There is no one optimal point.

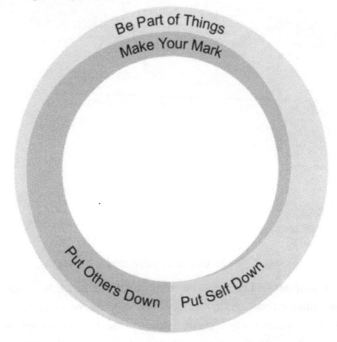

Figure 1 Ring of Preferences

**Ring of Support and Challenge**

Here's a small exercise I'd like you to do. Thinking of your relationships with those for whom you have responsibility, distribute 20 points between support and challenge. For, example, you might give 12 to support and 8 to challenge. Now multiply your two numbers. For example, 8 x 12 = 96. Make a note of your score now and I'll explain what it means soon.

Support and challenge can be represented as spirals within a ring. See Figure 2 below.

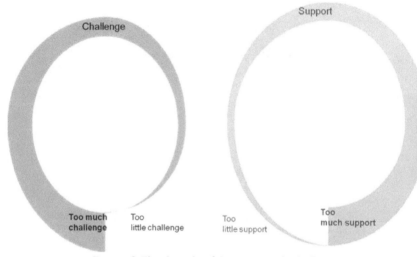

Figure 2 The Spirals of Support and Challenge

If support and challenge were mutually exclusive we could add their effect together to get their cumulative impact. But they are not mutually exclusive. Because the two forces impinge on each other, the quality of impact of our leadership, in parenting or teaching, for example equates to *support multiplied by challenge*. This means that we can't make up for deficiencies in one by maximising the other. We need both support and challenge in balance, one moderating the other. Being low on one approach actually undermines the other. For example, too much challenge with too little support creates an over-demanding coercion, causing psychological threat. This can then undermine the individuals we are supposedly there to help.

This was the all too common outcome in the authoritarian structures of the past. However, too much support combined with insufficient challenge forms an under-demanding collusion, leading to apathy. More importantly it can unwittingly undermine resilience.

Figure 3 presents support and challenge as complementary forces. Any mix within the upper half of the Ring is healthy and adaptive. The lower half illustrates how the mix has become imbalanced in one of two directions, either towards being over-demanding or over-protective.

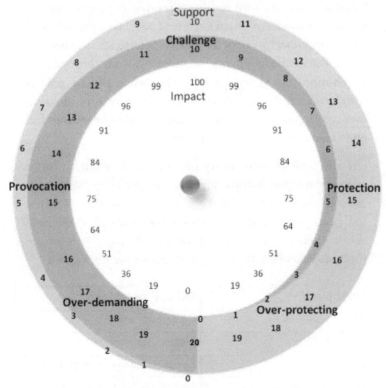

Figure 3 The Ring of Support and Challenge

The paired numbers on the spirals always add up to 20, but their product (shown inside the ring) will vary from 0 to 100 reflecting the multiplied impact of support and challenge on young people. The proud teacher or youth worker who rated her or himself as 17 for challenge needs to realise that the quality of impact (51) is reduced by the lack of support thereby putting him/her in the bottom or dark side of the Ring.

We can provoke to get a reaction, which can be for better or for worse, and we can protect learners to help meet their needs or to meet our own needs. Whenever we slip out of a workable balance, when our own needs eclipse young people's needs, we have a negative impact. One of the main purposes of education, either formal or informal, is helping learners become self-sufficient and independent. There is no long-term value in over-supporting young people who, when the support is withdrawn, crash and burn. But equally there is no point in over-challenging them as this will generate negative feelings and often lead them to feel overwhelmed.

If we have responsibility for others we need to build relationships that balance support and challenge. We do this through what I like to call the four WISE principles: Warmth, Independence, Sharing-the-reins and Encouragement. The table below illustrates how these principles help us to meet the psychological needs of those for whom we are responsible.

| Principle | Others' need for |
| --- | --- |
| **W**armth | Fitting in to seek acceptance |
| **I**ndependence | Making our mark, to achieve status |
| **S**haring-the-reins | Being part of things, to feel valued |
| **E**ncouragement | Making progress, to achieve |

Two of the principles relate to support and two to challenge:

**Support** involves validating and accepting young people for who they are, through:

- **Warmth** We are approachable and create a climate where people feel they can be themselves. We show a non-judgemental attitude that invites students to explore and express their identity without fear of disapproval. This creates a secure climate where young people feel safe to contribute and risk making mistakes.

- **Sharing-the-reins** We maximise a sense of common purpose and shared identity, through partnership, fun, humour and banter. We show curiosity about and connect with young people's interests, aspirations, concerns and opinions and we are open to exchanging feedback and being influenced by them. We invite young people's contribution as a valued partner.

**Challenge** means stretching young people, through:

- **Encouragement** This comes from personalised, achievable and specific goals. It inspires people's curiosity and fires their passions. We help individuals to recognise their efforts, strengths and areas for growth. We share expectations and information in order to let young people work out how they're progressing. We make them feel responsible for their progress. We give them a vision of who they can become. Encouragement is literally putting courage into the learner to stretch themselves.

- **Independence** Providing a structure with appropriate boundaries that affirms responsibility and accountability, fosters independence and strengthens personal identity. We give opportunities

for choices, decision-making, risk taking and learning
from mistakes. Independence can also involve
criticism and demand for more effort.

These four principles are inter-related and complementary. If we improve on one, we will enhance the others. Conversely, each principle would be diminished if we neglect any of the other three. A learning context without warmth creates a sense of disconnection. A lack of encouragement leaves learners apathetic. A learning environment devoid of sharing leads to selfishness. A lack of independence causes acquiescence or rebellion.

As leaders, parents and teachers we are never in neutral. We are either energising or draining our colleagues, children or students, benefiting or hindering them. When we support and challenge young people, we are validating and stretching their identity. When we are coldly demanding or warmly smothering we are threatening or restricting their identity. The four WISE principles function as *identity primers* that match the four motives.

Most of us instinctively provide warmth and encouragement; we are caring and keen for others to do well. These foundational principles enable us to develop the kind of relationships that make young people care about what we think of them. Sharing-the-reins and fostering independence requires a relationship that allows the direction of influence to work both ways. The task for us is to view young people as partners who have ownership of their learning. If we want learners to be respons-ible for their learning, we need to put them in control. Fostering independence and sharing-the-reins are more demanding but crucial because they communicate what we actually think of learners and, as such, are the principles that have greatest impact on young people's identities. The principles apply not just to individual learners but to our relationship with the whole group.

**Styles of influence**

How do you think people would describe you? Cold and distant? Scary? Friendly and enthusiastic? Someone who inspires respect? A bit of a pushover? A good laugh but not someone to take seriously? It is our *style* that determines our effectiveness as leaders, parents or teachers. And this is in large part down to how we affect others. Our style mediates in part our authority and, in particular, how much autonomy we support in others. Our style is communicated through our attitudes. An adult's attitude towards young people is one of the first things they notice when they first meet, and this perception is critical in creating their initial, and probably, lasting impressions.

I have designed free, online profiles to help us as leaders, teachers and parents to reflect on how we balance support and challenge. I have developed this Ring to facilitate greater objectivity and insight into ourselves and others. The online self-profiling tools offer carefully constructed feedback.

This Ring is sub-divided into sections which represent the styles, as you can see in Figure 4 below. Three styles are positive and seven are defensive. I have given them labels that represent the prominent characteristic of each style. However, it is important to realise that we are likely to move between these depending on circumstances, not least how we're feeling on any given day. Below I give information on some of the most common styles seen in those working with young people. Here I talk about youth workers, but these styles are also applicable to teachers, parents or anyone working with young people.

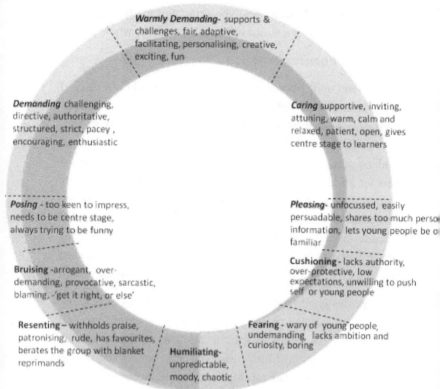

*Warmly Demanding*- supports & challenges, fair, adaptive, facilitating, personalising, creative, exciting, fun

*Demanding* challenging, directive, authoritative, structured, strict, pacey , encouraging, enthusiastic

*Caring* supportive, inviting, attuning, warm, calm and relaxed, patient, open, gives centre stage to learners

*Posing* - too keen to impress, needs to be centre stage, always trying to be funny

*Pleasing*- unfocussed, easily persuadable, shares too much personal information, lets young people be ol familiar

*Cushioning* - lacks authority, over-protective, low expectations, unwilling to push self or young people

*Bruising* -arrogant, over-demanding, provocative, sarcastic, blaming, 'get it right, or else'

*Resenting* – withholds praise, patronising, rude, has favourites, berates the group with blanket reprimands

*Fearing* - wary of young people, undemanding, lacks ambition and curiosity, boring

*Humiliating*- unpredictable, moody, chaotic

Figure 4 Styles of Influence

**The Positive Styles**

■ **Demanding** This pushy style prioritises challenge over support. Such youth workers are goal orientated and set high standards and expectations. Their enthusiasm and drive for success is infectious. As they give priority to progress they may be reluctant to make allowances for individual vulnerabilities. The demanding style can be effective as long as it is accompanied by warmth. But as soon as it is combined with toxins such as judgemental criticism,

indifference or arrogance, the youth worker may be
respected but feared or even hated.

- **Caring** This warm style prioritises support over
challenge, making young people feel accepted and
comfortable. Such youth workers take an invitational
approach and are wary of putting pressure on
individuals. They are kind, approachable and
reassuring and relate in a calm and patient manner.
However, there is a danger that people adopting this
style give priority to young people's problems over
their development. Similarly a caring style is effective
only if the person is efficient, knowledgeable and
skilled. Young people are likely to see caring without
competence as weak.

- **Warmly demanding** This style optimally blends
both support and challenge, reflecting the youth
worker's humility and ability to adapt flexibly to get it
right for each individual and ensure that goals are
met. They are tight on standards but know when to
exert pressure and when to ease off. With their pitch
perfect mix of authority and diplomacy they have the
capacity to reprimand people without belittling them.
The warmth of their support sets the foundation that
allows them to challenge young people in a way that
builds individual and collective pride.

## The Defensive Styles

We adopt defensive styles when we feel threatened, or when
our own needs crowd out our capacity to respond to others'
needs. Here I outline the most common defensive styles in youth
work or teaching.

- **Pleasing** This style tries to accommodate
everyone's needs but the slow progress frustrates
those around them. The worker's self-doubt can

make them indecisive and hard to take seriously and they struggle to assert their authority. Their pleasing style promises a lot but often fails to deliver. They try to help too much, like an over-attentive waiter or a 'helicopter parent'.

■ **Cushioning** The cushioning youth worker may fail to set clear goals and boundaries, be *laissez-faire* in their approach, let young people be over familiar, or sidestep challenging feedback. This saccharine style gives unmerited praise and so creates dependency or apathy. The youth worker's own vulnerability is contagious and undermines the collective sense of security or cohesion.

■ **Fearing** With this style the youth worker is fearful of challenging young people. This undemanding style is inhibiting. Such a pedestrian style communicates a lack of direction, ambition and confidence. Such workers give little feedback and their low commitment rubs off on young people who, in turn, don't try too hard because nobody will appreciate it anyway!

■ **Posing** In this mode the youth worker's priority is to grandstand and display his or her expertise rather than develop their charges. They see the group as an audience to impress. Posing individuals tend to talk too much, in particular about themselves, and are quick to credit themselves for any success. They may try to be funny but their miscued humour has the opposite effect.

We can probably relate to elements of all of these styles from our own experience of leaders. A more challenging question is whether we see ourselves in some of them. It is important to realise that different people need a different approach. Some need to be pushed, others need a metaphorical hug. It is most productive if we try to operate within the positive styles but we should also forgive ourselves and move on when we have lapsed into the defensive styles. The more we are aware of our default 'good day' style and its strengths as well as the 'bad day' style we might adopt when stressed or threatened, the better placed we are to give the best of ourselves and get the best from others.

Young people who prefer *being part of things* and enjoy connecting emotions such as gratitude and concern for others, have a potential to be threatened by excessive demands or fear of rejection or disapproval. They may subsequently be hard on themselves and experience emotions like self-doubt or shame. Others whose preference is for *'making our mark'* will more likely enjoy stretching emotions like pride and determination. They have the potential to be stressed by a loss of control or any barriers erected to their independence. They then react defensively with conflicting emotions such as arrogance or resentment.

We can also use the Ring of Support and Challenge to chart the range of climates in any learning setting, as displayed in Figure 5 below. For simplicity, I describe the climates with reference mainly to classrooms and teachers.

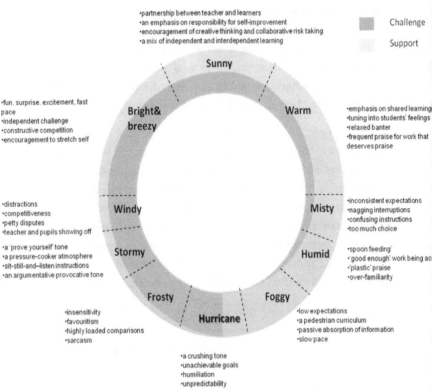

Figure 5 The Climates

In any culture, making our mark, in the form of freedom to initiate action, is the grease that drives improvement, innovation and change. Individuals pushing themselves to improve generate an infectious pressure that pushes everyone. However, when this predominates, inequality, conflict and favouritism undermine trust and any sense of common purpose. An unhealthy culture of individualism takes hold. Only some can thrive. Inequality damages relationships, heightens status anxieties and triggers unhealthy competition. Ideally, being part of things provides the glue that creates a unified culture which, in turn, empowers but holds in check making our mark. It can't happen the other way around. A flourishing culture capitalises on the positive emotions that flow from personal and collective progress.

Shared autonomy is what makes colleagues pull together and maximises collective agency and innovation. It is the life-blood of healthy cultures, and makes it possible for everyone, individually and collectively, to achieve more. Working together, and in workable balance, the spirals of shared and personal autonomy create a culture of 'collective ambition'. Culture has to be in our hearts and our hearts have to be in the culture.

In conclusion, providing warmth and sharing-the-reins give the nutrients of support for young people's connecting emotions and identities. Through warm, non-judgmental relationships we show that we care about others and want to get to know them as individuals. Because belonging is our deepest need, support is an essential precursor to challenge. The quality of our support will determine how receptive others are to our challenge. But without the stretch provided by challenge, support risks becoming a form of over-protection. Offering encouragement and fostering independence create challenge. Challenge offers the catalyst for people's stretching emotions and expands their identities. It starts with an authoritative structure that sets limits but allows people to express their individuality and stretches them to maximise their talents. However, without the balance provided by support, challenge can be threatening.

This brings us back again to the need for balance between support and challenge. Back to Aristotle and his wise words on finding the golden mean. □

# From One Extreme to Another: Parenting in Scotland

Carol Craig

> Carol Craig is the Chief Executive of the Centre for Confidence
> and Well-being and the series editor for *Postcards from Scotland*.
> Carol has written extensively on confidence and well-being. She
> is the author of *The Scots' Crisis of Confidence, The Tears that
> Made the Clyde, Creating Confidence, The Great Takeover* and
> *Hiding in Plain Sight*. She has spent much of the last fifteen years
> discussing and writing about young people's resilience and
> confidence. She has two sons and three grandsons.

WHEN I was growing up in the 1950s and 60s Scotland still had
a punitive and authoritarian culture. This was particularly
evident in the home. Children were expected to obey rules but
they were rarely explained. If we dared to question we were
simply told 'because I say so'. Many of us were also subject to
frequent criticism and received little praise. When we did
something wrong we were often humiliated or shamed. We
weren't encouraged to speak out or express our opinions.
Indeed we were often told that we should be seen and not heard.

Punishment was also harsh. Most parents smacked or sometimes beat their offspring. Teachers routinely belted children
not just for gross indiscipline but also trivial misdemeanours
and even academic mistakes. It was only when I was undertaking
research for my latest book *Hiding in Plain Sight: Exploring
Scotland's ill health* that I discovered that Scotland's use of
corporal punishment was not only excessive but exceptional.

Evidence suggests that state schools in Scotland used corporal punishment more than their equivalents in England and Wales. Hitting primary school children was rare in England but commonplace in Scotland. The majority of European countries outlawed corporal punishment in the early part of the twentieth century if not before. Scotland was effectively forced to stop belting children in state schools in 1987 as a result of an edict from the European Court of Human Rights. This happened as a result of an appeal by two Scottish mothers.

The fact that Scotland was forced to abandon corporal punishment by an external agency is significant: there has never been a Scotland wide campaign explaining why hitting children is not just morally wrong but counterproductive. Scots have never publicly discussed how to promote responsible behaviour.

There are still some signs of this punitive Old Testament view of the world in contemporary Scotland. In some surveys a majority of Scots respondents support the return of capital punishment. Over 50 countries in the world have outlawed parental smacking of children but a ComRes survey reported recently that two-thirds of Scottish respondents were opposed to such legislation being introduced here.

But, paradoxically, for me the legacy of Scotland's authoritarian past is the ubiquity of indulgent, over-protective parenting. Scottish parenting has gone from one extreme to another. This matters for young people's resilience and well-being. It also matters for academic success.

### Changes in child-rearing and education

I had a very loving mother but for reasons I set out in *Hiding in Plain Sight* I had a miserable and often painful childhood. When my first son was born I consciously resolved that he would never experience any unhappiness and pain. In short, I wanted to protect him from the negative experiences of my own childhood.

I was not alone in harbouring a strong desire to protect my son from the way I had been treated as a child. For sixteen years in the 1980s and 90s I ran a large number of personal development courses involving thousands and thousands of people, the vast majority of whom were Scots. In the course of our discussions many would say that while they loved their parents and felt indebted to them, they had often been harsh, cold and excessively critical. There was little encouragement or praise. Many participants also reported that their parents were physically undemonstrative. Like me they resolved to bring their children up differently. They weren't just going to hug them and tell them repeatedly that they were loved, they were also going to shower them with compliments and praise. And they were not going to let teachers punish or talk negatively to their children.

So in a nutshell Scots of my generation (and later) vowed to bring up their children differently. This was a quiet revolution which happened behind closed doors and without public discussion. There was no 'Truth and Reconciliation' process to help us get over the punitive years of Scotland's traditional approach to child-rearing. We simply moved on.

I might never have thought more of these conversations if it had not been for Professor Martin Seligman, one of the world's leading psychologists. In 2003 he was in Scotland to speak at a conference I was helping to organise in the wake of the publication of my book *The Scots' Crisis of Confidence*. During a private conversation Seligman said: 'Make sure you stick to confidence and don't go down the self-esteem route. This is what has happened in the US and it's toxic.'

Within a few months I set up the Centre for Confidence and Well-being and Scottish schools were presented with a new Curriculum for Excellence with its emphasis on the importance of creating 'confident individuals'. So I heeded Seligman's warning and looked in-depth at the allegations that the self-esteem movement in America was undermining both young people's well-being and their academic achievements. I then wrote *Creating Confidence: A handbook for professionals working with young people* to share some of what I had learned on how well-meaning overprotectiveness can be taken too far and how a fixation with how children were feeling in the moment was not good for children's well-being or learning.

Once the book was published I ran lots of workshops for teachers on confidence in which I outlined the dangers of the self-esteem approach. Teachers specifically told me that what I described as commonplace practices in the US were also happening here in Scotland.

In America's case the massive change in education and child-rearing happened as a result of a highly influential self-esteem movement which presented self-esteem boosting as a panacea. Educators naturally took notice of these claims and promoting self-esteem became the core mission of most American schools. Parents too started to believe that they also had to boost their children's self-esteem.

In Scotland there was no vocal self-esteem movement arguing for a change in approach to rearing children yet we drifted in this direction nonetheless. And this takes me back to that quiet revolution that was taking place in Scotland. That steely determination that many parents had to bring up their children differently and to ensure that their children were treated better at school than they had been. But sadly, just as in the US, this new style of treating children ushered in new unspoken problems.

**Parenting styles**

As the impetus in Scotland for an excessively protective and positive approach came originally from parents, not schools, it is worth looking at different ways parents can behave towards their children. In the 1960s the American developmental psychologist Diana Baumrind observed young children and pronounced that there were three styles of parenting – authoritarian, authoritative, and permissive (sometimes called indulgent). Later researchers added a fourth style – neglectful or uninvolved.

These four styles, set out in Table 1, have been supported by considerable research and still influence parent education. Before explaining what each type looks like it is worth pointing out that parents don't always stick with one style and can move from one to another. And this can present serious problems for children as it means their lives are unpredictable. Unpredictability is a major source of toxic stress for children, a term we'll return to later.

Table 1: Parenting styles

| **Authoritarian** | **Authoritative** |
|---|---|
| Cold and firm | Warm and firm |
| **Neglectful/uninvolved** | **Permissive/indulgent** |
| Cold and soft | Warm and soft |

These styles echo Alan McLean's work on 'classroom climate' and in his article in this book he defines authoritative as 'warmly demanding'.

### The neglectful style

The worst style for children's emotional health and future academic success is neglectful or uninvolved. As I explain in *The Tears that Made the Clyde* and *Hiding in Plain Sight* Scotland had more than its fair share of neglectful fathers. Scotland's infamous slum housing drove many men out of the house to drink and socialise and many had little time for their families. Some would provide the bare necessities for children such as food or shelter but they would offer little in the way of emotional input or even rules. You could do what you liked because your neglectful father didn't care. Except when he came home one night, drunk and suddenly objected to what you were doing. . .

Neglectful parenting is still an issue in contemporary Scotland. Some parents are too distressed by their own problems to be good parents or they simply don't know how to look after children because their own parents were inadequate. But it is wrong to see this as exclusively a problem of people living in poor communities. As Alan Sinclair argues so persuasively in his book *Right from the Start* many middle-class parents can be too busy with their own careers or lives to be good parents to their children. One in four children who are deemed 'vulnerable' when they start school in Scotland have middle class or wealthy parents. I have spoken to a number of people working in private schools in Scotland who report that many of their pupils feel emotionally neglected by their parents. This is also reflected in the private nursery sector where children may be in nursery from 8am to 6pm, having all their meals away from the family.

### *The authoritarian style*

The authoritarian parenting style is also not good for young people and it's this style which usually prevailed in the Scotland of my youth. Research clearly shows that, at least in Western countries, authoritarian (*cold* and *firm*) parenting undermines children and young people's emotional development. As their behaviour is constantly being manipulated by external threats or punishments their intrinsic motivation is often weak and this can therefore reduce their academic performance and overall sense of self-efficacy. Children with authoritarian parents are not expected to put forward arguments but just do what they are told, so their ability to communicate and express themselves is often undermined. As parental validation is often withheld, and they can be subjected to excessive criticism and humiliation, such children often lack confidence or self-esteem. What's more they can become dependent on others for validation or approval. However, depending on personality, they can also become aggressive and rebellious. The future mental health of people brought up by authoritarian parents can be compromised and some studies link authoritarian parenting with future depression, although this may depend on the degree of parental coldness.

### *The authoritative style*

Extensive research shows that the best type of parenting for children is authoritative. What this means is that the parent is child-centred, loving and focused on the child's welfare but has clear rules and boundaries. Such parents let their children know what's expected but they are also prepared to reason with them – explaining and discussing the rules. Authoritative parents take their children's feelings into account when making decisions and also ask their children to talk about how they feel. They deliberately try to foster independence and responsibility. Authoritative parenting can be described as *warm and firm* in that it is both responsive and demanding.

Research shows that for children from European or American backgrounds authoritative parenting is best as it encourages the development of healthy characteristics such as self-control and autonomy. It also helps to foster positive mental health. Children and adolescents with authoritative parents generally perform better academically than those with parents who adopt different styles. Indeed a systematic literature review of 131 papers on parenting styles and academic achievement concluded that 'Authoritative parenting tends to promote better and positive outcomes in child development.'

### *The permissive style*
Permissive parents are very involved with their children but they don't place many restrictions on them and don't exercise discipline. They dislike saying 'no' to their children and so indulge them. They are nurturing and child focused and, in the absence of any boundaries, the child is allowed to make decisions.

The children of permissive parents benefit from their parents' warmth, love and interest in them but they suffer from the lack of rules or boundaries. As a result such children struggle to learn self-control and do not have such good psychosocial skills as peers with authoritative parents. Research cited earlier shows that they do not do as well at school as children with authoritative parents. Research also suggests that those who pile on certain types of praise on their children (such as 'you are so clever or talented') may, unwittingly, undermine their willingness to take risks or stretch themselves.

Indulgent parenting also tends to be overprotective of the child's feelings. Such parents don't want their child to have an unhappy thought or negative experience so they go out of their way to ensure that nothing of this type happens.

## Parenting styles in Scotland

Some of the parents in Scotland who deliberately decided not to emulate their own parents adopted an authoritative style. But as far as I can see they were a small minority. One explanation is simply that the predominance of strong authoritarian parenting meant there were very few examples of authoritative parenting to copy. I can think of only one girl in my primary school class with parents like this and they were left-leaning intellectuals. What's more, in wider Scottish society – education and the prevailing work culture in particular – there wasn't an ethos of negotiation or compromise to learn from. This was the land of the 'wee hard men' to use the artist and novelist Alasdair Gray's term. In Scotland people were (and still are to some extent) just 'tellt'.

In my experience the parents who wanted to be different from their parents went from a style that was *cold* and *firm* to one that is *warm* and *soft*. In short, they didn't move towards the authoritative style: they became permissive or indulgent. This type of parenting is often very loving and child-focused and is certainly better than the old authoritarian style but it generates its own problems.

Over the years I have had the privilege of discussing young people's confidence, resilience and well-being with lots of teachers, head teachers and parents. From these discussions I know that many parents are intent on protecting their children from any emotional challenge. Many parents have a belief (which I once held) that children shouldn't experience negative feelings as it will undermine them and be too difficult to cope with. Here are a few telling examples:

■ A mother coming in to school to complain that her child didn't get the lead part in the pantomime and is so upset that she feels they are being cruel to him.

■ A Director of Education pursued by a father who said it was her job to deal with the fact that his daughter was the only girl in the class not to be invited to a party happening outside school hours.

■ A mother who complained to me privately at a parents' evening that the teacher shouldn't be teaching the class how to spell 'father' as her daughter's father had died some months before.

As life inevitably involves loss, challenge and hurt feelings it is not actually possible to protect children from negative emotions. More importantly this is not only an unrealistic goal it's actually not good for children. Bad feelings have a purpose – they are a source of guidance. They also galvanise us to do things differently. Of course, we can sympathise with the wee girl who wasn't invited to the birthday party but she has to fathom out what she might be doing that is alienating potential friends. Perhaps she needs to change her behaviour and this may be a lesson best learned early in life. And the girl who lost her father will never be able to avoid hearing the word.

The tragedy for parents is that in the long run it's exhausting to think that you must always protect your children from negative feelings. Not only do you undermine your child in the process, you are also destined to fail and feel inadequate.

Another worrying issue is the way that many parents think that any learning challenge is too much for their child to bear and should be avoided. In short they equate challenge with dangerous stress. Yet learning anything worth learning is frustrating and often challenging. What's more, observational research with caregivers of pre-school children found that development was quicker for those children who were repeatedly given feedback on the challenging nature of the activity in which they were involved. Children whose caregivers gave them praise for accomplishing easy tasks progressed at a slower rate.

Professor Carol Dweck, of Mindset fame, is now fond of saying that we need to redeem the idea of struggle and challenge. We need to get away from the idea that easy praise and easy tasks are beneficial to youngsters' development. They aren't. So it's worrying that school staff have repeatedly told me about parents writing to secondary teachers to say that they shouldn't try to teach their child French (or maths, music or sport) because 'they can't do it and it's stressing them'.

The idea that challenge is bad is most damaging for young people from poor backgrounds. If they don't learn first time round they don't get another chance. Middle class youngsters' failure to learn is rectified or masked by input from more educated parents or tutors.

We also need to recognise that challenge is an important part of feelings of satisfaction and fulfilment. For example, youngsters involved in the Duke of Edinburgh Award will often complain volubly during the expedition part of the scheme that the journey is too arduous. Yet it is the expedition which they will then say was most important and memorable. As Alan McLean argues cogently in his article apathy often results from removing challenge from young people's lives.

Scientists have now shown that children's health is undermined if they are not exposed to germs as this retards the immune system. So it is perfectly understandable that young people's psychological immune system – their resilience – can be weakened if they do not face adversities and have challenging experiences. Children can only learn that they can cope if they meet challenges and manage to bounce back. Part of the process of building resilience is encouraging youngsters to see challenges, setbacks, failures and everyday adversities as a normal part of life. Interestingly one drama teacher told me that young people now often say they can't speak in class because they feel 'anxious'. 'What they fail to understand,' she said, 'is that when it comes to drama and lots of other things in life anxiety is normal.'

Of course, young people should be supported through challenges. Indeed having a network of support is a key aspect of resilience. But adults have to be aware of the difference between supporting young people through challenges and trying to prevent them from ever experiencing 'difficult' feelings.

Another issue is parents not being able to say 'no' to their children. Pre-school and primary teachers have told me about youngsters being so tired that they are falling asleep in class and parents saying that they don't know how to get their child to go to bed. Other teachers say they are shocked at the junk that many parents put in their children's lunch boxes. Of course we should encourage children to become independent, make decisions for themselves and have a sense of agency but they need to exercise their independence within clearly delineated boundaries.

Many parents now take the view that children know what's best and that they are being child-centred in letting them make decisions for themselves. But this is not in children's long-term interests. Children's minds are heavily influenced by daily exposure to advertising. It's parents who have to set standards for food, bedtimes and screen time. Parents imperil their children's future by indulging them and always letting them do what they want. It simply isn't a good strategy for parents to try to be their child's 'best friend'.

I believe that the vast majority of parents want to do the best by their children and that, for perfectly understandable reasons, they are now overly concerned about anything negative or difficult in their children's lives. But life could be better for parents, and their children, if they could get over their own fears of negative or difficult feelings.

Parenting need not be so problematic, even in contemporary times. An in-depth piece of qualitative research by Professor Agnes Nairn showed that in Sweden, the country with the highest child well-being, parents are loving and child-centred but they define their role as bringing up children to be 'independent'. They expect young children to do chores, they don't buy them a lot of consumer goods and they think a 'deprived child' is one who has little contact with nature. I have little doubt that the relative equality of Sweden plays an important part in their child well-being but these cultural factors also help. In Sweden they are able to be authoritative parents – to provide both warmth and boundaries.

**Adverse Childhood Experiences**

So how does all this fit with the growing emphasis in schools and youth organisations on 'Adverse Childhood Experiences' (ACEs)? There is undoubtedly mounting interest in this topic thanks to the work of inspirational women like Dr Suzanne Zeedyk and Pauline Scott who want Scotland to become 'the first ACE-aware nation'. As my recent book *Hiding in Plain Sight* focuses on the prevalence of ACEs in Scottish culture I welcome this development. Understanding the impact of trauma on young people and how it can affect their behaviour and ability to learn may be vital for pupils who are living through traumatic experiences. Hopefully it will help them get the emotional support they may need.

But it is important that educationalists and others continually make a distinction between ACEs and everyday adversities; between ordinary challenges and what Harvard University's Centre on the Developing Child calls 'toxic stress':

> This can occur when a child experiences strong, frequent, and/or prolonged adversity – such as physical or emotional abuse, chronic neglect, caregiver substance abuse or mental illness, exposure to violence, and/or the accumulated burdens of family economic hardship – without adequate adult support. This kind of prolonged activation of the stress response systems can disrupt the development of brain architecture and other organ systems, and increase the risk for stress-related disease and cognitive impairment, well into the adult years.

Jack Shonkoff, a professor in child health and development at Harvard, is clear that not all stress endured by children can be classified as 'toxic'. Indeed he writes about the 'positive stress response' which can lead to brief elevations in heart rate and stress hormones but which is an 'essential part of healthy development'. Time-limited stressors such as minor accidents, disagreements with friends, learning challenges would all fit into this definition of 'positive stress'. What's more, even when the child is exposed to numerous ACEs, the stress may be 'tolerable' if she or he is in a supportive relationship with one parent or caregiver.

We do not know what the prevalence rate for ACEs is for Scottish children but if it's similar to the rate in the USA or Wales then around half will experience no ACEs. These children will benefit from the absence of toxic stress but they could be undermined by too little difficulty in their childhood. Extensive empirical research conducted by Professor Mark Seery shows that children who experience moderate stress in early life fare better than those who had experienced no adversities in their childhood. He believes that negative or difficult life experiences early in life can help people develop an 'ability to cope'.

It will be a great pity if, as a result of the rising interest in ACEs, teachers and parents become even more protective, thereby undermining youngsters' resilience further. It will also be detrimental if parents become so alarmed at the prospect of stress damaging their children's health that they become anxious about upsetting them and then become even more indulgent and permissive. There is nothing in the ACE research which contradicts the evidence that authoritative parenting is best. Children don't only need love and affection but also clear rules and boundaries.

Dr Suzanne Zeedyk, a developmental psychologist, is aware of these issues. Indeed she has written about parenting styles.

She thinks that if parents avoid confronting hurt from their own childhood they can easily become overly anxious about their children experiencing painful feelings. She does not think that trying to protect children from all negative emotion is good for their development.

Children's resilience is built from learning that life inevitably has emotionally challenging moments, and that there is someone to call on for help during such moments. Resilience can't be built through avoiding those challenges. According to Suzanne Zeedyk:

> These are issues that the Scottish ACE movement is helping us, indeed forcing us, to confront. The first step in the movement has been to make people aware that emotional experiences affect biology. One challenge now is for us to distinguish between stress and toxic stress. It won't help our children or families if we confuse the two. The science of ACEs shows us that stress turns toxic when children have to handle hard times alone, because they end up feeling overwhelmed. It is up to us adults to realise that, for healthy development, children really do need emotional challenges, but they also need to know that they can seek help when the challenges feel too tough. Help is different from protection.

## Scotland wide effects of the shift in parenting style

We can already see how overprotective, permissive parenting is having a negative health impact on Scotland's children. Last year an international survey of 38 countries on children's physical activity ranked Scotland joint last even though the country scored second top for national policy on physical activity. What children do at school is obviously important but the report's author Professor John Reilly has said that protective parents stopping kids from being physically active outdoors in Scotland is part of the problem. Scotland was also joint first on the amount of time children spent watching screens and this is partly a reflection of parental permissiveness – a failure to set healthy limits and boundaries. Other parts of the UK did not score well either but they were still ahead of Scotland. Interestingly one Edinburgh primary head teacher told me recently that more parents will get in touch to complain about their child having to endure a wet playtime than will turn up at an event to talk about internet safety. Yet this is a real threat as even P3 children at the school are accessing inappropriate material online.

The lack of exercise and play for Scottish children is an important issue. When I have spoken to parents at school events about overprotection and a fear of negative experiences they always link what I am saying to two things: how parents commonly restrict their children's freedom to play outdoors and how they allow youngsters to stay indoors and be involved with different kinds of media. As Sue Palmer argues cogently in her article in this book, self-directed outdoor play is vital for young people's emotional well-being and social skills.

And what of education itself? In the last few years it has become clear that something is seriously amiss. The Scottish Government's own figures show that since 2011 standards in literacy and numeracy have fallen. Scotland's place has also declined in international league tables. Since 2006 Scotland's place in the OECD's 'PISA' rankings have dropped for the three core subjects – reading, maths and science. Scotland's yawning attainment gap between rich and poor children is not closing.

As permissive parenting does not support good academic

outcomes it's possible that parenting style is at least *a part* of Scotland's growing educational challenge. I'm emphatically not blaming parents for all the ills of Scotland's children or the yawning attainment gap. Poverty and inequality play a huge part in this. Curriculum changes may have contributed and so too what's happening in our schools.

The Scottish Government has taken a heavy-handed approach to falling standards and the attainment gap. They plan structural change to schooling and have also introduced national testing for all children in P1. I am all for challenge in schools but not this challenge! I'm totally opposed to the testing of four and five-year-olds. As a passionate Upstart supporter (and Board member) I would like to see the under-sevens immersed in outdoor play. As well as providing routine challenges, play based education gives children a sense of agency and some control over their own development. It is also the norm in most European countries.

In other respects local authorities and the Scottish Government are intent on removing different types of educational challenges. I have been informed by various teachers, both primary and secondary, that they are only expected to write positive reports for parents on their child's performance even if this is untrue. Some also express concern that parents are not adequately informed on how well their child is actually performing academically until S4.

Many teachers are parents themselves so they understand this contemporary drive to protect children's feelings but they also say that it makes their job impossible. By definition all the children in the class can't get the lead part in the pantomime or be popular with their classmates. Many teachers feel that the system is geared more to placate parents in their drive to protect their individual child than to support them as teachers or head teachers. These educationalists are not arguing for a return to the bad old days of Scottish education, which they acknowledge were punitive and draconian. But they think a better balance is required.

In a workshop last year a secondary teacher from the Netherlands had some interesting observations to make about Scottish schools. He argued that the prevailing atmosphere is 'too positive and too lenient'. He argued that in Holland young people have weekly challenges and more responsibility for their learning. This may sound tough but the Netherlands sits at the top of international league tables for child well-being and happiness. The Dutch teacher also argued that Scottish youngsters don't have enough challenges. They are not encouraged to stretch themselves enough or strive. In the same workshop many Scottish teachers said that there was too much 'spoon feeding' and that deadlines for homework were now almost meaningless. Someone involved in organising study visits to Scotland for Chinese headteachers reports that they are always asking 'when is the pressure applied?'

Undoubtedly some schools and education authorities are trying to tackle the issues I've raised here in meetings with parents. I know this because I've been asked to speak at various parents' evenings in one local authority. Another videoed one of my talks so they could transmit it to lots of schools in their area. Schools pursuing the *Bounce Back!* programme, designed to boost youngsters' resilience, also routinely talk about some of these issues with parents. But they are the minority. These issues have yet to be publicly acknowledged.

**A generational shift . . .**

Of course, this shift from authoritarian parenting hasn't only happened in Scotland. This is a generational change that you can identify elsewhere. But because Scotland had a particularly punitive culture, the counter reaction here may have been stronger than in countries like Italy, Spain or the Netherlands with a long history of a more child-centred approach. In Sweden the move has been to an authoritative style. Parents in America, Australia, New Zealand and the rest of the UK have grappled with similar issues to the ones I have outlined here. 'Helicopter parenting' is the term that's often used.

It is now commonplace for young people to be referred to as 'Generation Snowflake'. This refers not just to a lack of resilience but to a propensity to take offence much more easily than previous generations. Critics refer to the widespread use of 'trigger warnings' on US campuses, giving students prior warning of material they may find challenging, the demand for 'safe spaces' and to the way that people with contrary views are not allowed to express their opinions.

I have no sense that these are particular issues for us in Scotland. But I do think we have a strong notion of human fragility and that this is undermining resilience and educational performance as we attempt to protect young people from any difficult or challenging experiences. Given our history of authoritarianism both at home and at school until the 1980s many parents were bound to react strongly – to take whatever action to defend and protect their children from similar experiences. But sadly many have gone from one extreme to another – from authoritarian to indulgent and permissive. When it comes to child-rearing there is indeed 'a golden mean'.  □

# The Silence of the Weans

Sue Palmer

A former primary headteacher in the Scottish Borders, Sue Palmer is an independent writer and consultant on primary education, particularly literacy. Her book *Toxic Childhood* illustrates the latest research from around the world on a range of problem areas. These include poor diet, lack of exercise, sleep deprivation and other difficulties that are currently having a major effect on young people's health and well-being. In this chapter Sue highlights the importance of play for children and its implications for their social and emotional development to enable them to acquire social skills and a sense of social responsibility through personal experience. Sue is the Chair of Upstart Scotland.

SIXTY years ago, people walking in American country lanes noticed the birds had stopped singing. Their concern led to a book, *Silent Spring* by Rachel Carson, explaining how crop-spraying of DDT killed wildlife and wrecked the local ecology. As well as securing a ban on dangerous pesticides, publicity around *Silent Spring* brought the environmental movement to public attention.

Perhaps you've noticed that, over the last couple of decades, another sound has disappeared from our daily environment? When was the last time you heard the shouts, squeals and laughter of young children as they ran, jumped, climbed, built dens, made mixtures and played 'Let's Pretend' in their local neighbourhood?

Upstart Scotland is a campaign aimed at focusing public attention on serious changes in the nature of childhood that are already having dangerous repercussions. The most significant of these changes is the decline of outdoor free play.

There isn't one simple reason that children don't play out any more. The build-up of road traffic, the breakdown of local communities and changes in parents' working patterns are all implicated, as are the ready availability of indoor sedentary entertainment and a generally more fearful climate (probably related to occasional horrifying media stories about abduction).

But the reason we should be concerned about this loss **is** simple. Active outdoor play is a biological necessity for long-term physical and mental health. As play has declined, we've seen more and more cases of childhood obesity, Vitamin D deficiency and other physical conditions with alarming long-term implications for the National Health Service.

Perhaps even more alarming is the increase in mental health problems among children and young people – now reaching crisis point in Scotland. An article in the November 2017 edition of the medical journal *The Lancet* pointed out the links between this swelling tide and the decline of outdoor free play.

**Why play matters**

The reason it's taken so long to recognise this emergency is that – from an adult perspective – play doesn't seem anywhere near as important as education. We see it as just kids messing about. And how can what wee ones do when left to their own devices be of any significance? Yet the evidence now emerging from neuroscience and evolutionary biology suggests that play actually has immense significance, not only for health and well-being, but for educational success.

In fact, play is children's inborn learning drive – it's how evolution has primed them to develop human capacities they'll need to flourish throughout life. 'Messing about', especially in the great outdoors, develops children's powers of creativity, adaptability and problem-solving. It's how they hone their social skills of communication and collaboration with their peers, and – through making up rules for their own games and activities – how they come to understand the need for shared rules, regulations and conventions. And it's also essential for the development of personal qualities like perseverance, self-control and the emotional resilience that we all need for long-term mental health and well-being.

These qualities and capacities can't be taught – either by teachers at school or computers at home – they have to **develop** in each individual child's body and brain, in the holistic way decreed by evolution over countless millennia.

So does another crucial capacity that develops gradually during the early years: self-regulation. This is the ability to control one's own emotions and behaviour and it's essential if children are to benefit from formal schooling. Self-regulation involves – among other things – the gradual development of physical coordination, social knowhow, memory skills, empathy and the ability to make rapid decisions and adapt behaviour to changing circumstances. Play provides endless opportunities for practising self-regulation skills.

This isn't to say, of course, that the adults who care for children don't have an important role in their physical, social, emotional and cognitive development. Not only are adult carers responsible for keeping the younger generation safe and providing for their material needs, but from the moment children are born they act as models for social behaviour, pass on communication skills and supervise the environment in which play happens. Perhaps most important of all, they also provide the unconditional loving support that underpins a child's sense of personal confidence, self-worth and self-respect.

But an important part of that loving support is knowing when to back off. If adults over-supervise and over-direct children's play, there's a serious danger that their charges will fail to develop a sense of personal agency and self-efficacy, qualities that are just as essential for long-term self-regulation skills and emotional resilience as confidence, self-worth and self-respect. Play provides opportunities for every growing child to discover his or her own strengths, to experiment with small manageable risks, to learn through trial and error how to cope with setbacks, to rise to challenges and bounce back from difficulties.

The need for adults to 'back off' during play can be accounted for in terms of our species' cultural evolution. For most of human history contraception didn't exist so, by the age of two or three, the overwhelming majority of children would be supplanted in their mother's attention by a new baby. The 'old baby' (now independent enough to cope) would become the responsibility of big brothers, sisters, cousins and so on, as they played out in the local community. Adults would still keep a weather eye on proceedings, but in every time and culture until the twentieth century, the overwhelming majority of young children had a great deal of freedom to play and, as they grew older, a fair degree of responsibility for ensuring the well-being of their peers.

The implications of this for social and emotional development are clear. Personal social skills and a personal sense of social responsibility have, to a large extent, been acquired by children through the centuries as a result of personal experience. While adults can help the process along by modelling self-regulated behaviour and, hopefully, advising and supporting children in dealing with squabbles and fall-outs, the children also need time and space to internalise these skills through their own efforts. If grown-ups always rush in and sort out social problems that arise during play, we deprive the next generation of opportunities to develop the sense of personal agency and self-efficacy that underpins self-regulation, emotional resilience and intrinsic motivation to learn.

### 'The first seven years are for play'

Learning through play is particularly important in the first seven or so years, when children are establishing the neural networks that influence the whole of their lives. Throughout human history, the under-sevens have been regarded as 'infants', for whom play is the main activity. The Romans divided childhood into three seven-year chunks: *infans* (birth to seven), *pueri* (seven to 14), *adolescens* (14-21) and when formal schooling first became normalised (at least for wealthy, male children) by the Greeks and Romans, it began at age seven.

The prophet Mohammed echoed this chunking system: 'The first seven years are for play; the second seven are for discipline and education; the third are for keeping with the adults and being initiated into one's adult role.' There are similar sayings from other cultures, such as the Japanese proverb that 'The first seven years are the gods' domain.'

In 1837, when the educationist Frederick Froebel set up his Institute of Play and Activity for Small Children (the world's first 'kindergarten'), he too chose seven as the age at which children were ready for formal education, as did other great early years pioneers who followed him – such as Steiner, Montessori and Malaguzzi – and the two great twentieth century developmental psychologists, Piaget and Vygotsky.

Nowadays, the United Nations errs on the side of caution, defining 'early childhood' as the period from birth to eight years old – 'a time of remarkable growth with brain development at its peak. . . [when] children are highly influenced by the environment and the people that surround them.' High quality early childhood education and care (ECEC) is therefore based on well-established developmental principles, in which nurture and learning through play are prioritised, rather than a narrow focus on 'academic' skills. In most European countries, there is a kindergarten stage before formal schooling begins, for children from the age of three to six or seven.

Scotland is one of only four countries in Europe that sends its children to school at the age of four or five: the others are England, Wales and Northern Ireland. Indeed, only 12 per cent of countries worldwide start school so early. . . and all bar one are ex-members of the British empire. Our early school starting age was decided by the Westminster parliament in the late 1860s. It was deemed convenient to begin compulsory schooling as early as possible because it released mothers from childcare to work in the factories – and the sooner children began their education, the sooner they could finish and go to work in the factories too. Even at the time, four or five was considered by many parliamentarians to be too young for school. But the economic argument swung the vote and compulsory schooling, starting the year children turn five, has been the norm in Britain and much of the Commonwealth ever since.

## The state of play in Scotland

After 150 years, we take it for granted that children should start school – where we automatically assume they will get cracking on the three Rs – at the age of four or five. Yet, as outlined above, there's never been any educational justification for this very early school starting age and a number of international research studies have shown that beginning formal education before the age of six is not only educationally unnecessary but can, in some cases, have long-term negative consequences.

Nevertheless, there hasn't been widespread concern about the UK's early start policy until very recently. Perhaps one reason is that, until the turn of the last century, most children still had plenty of freedom to play: every evening, at weekends and during school holidays, four-, five- and six-year-olds would be out with their pals in the local streets, fields or wild places, making up for all that wasted time in the classroom. However, as that freedom has disappeared, it's increasingly apparent that – despite immense investment of money, time and professional expertise – the performance of early-start countries in international comparisons of achievement in literacy and numeracy has been distinctly lacklustre. There has also been a serious increase in developmental conditions and mental health problems.

It shouldn't, in fact, be the case in Scotland, where our *Curriculum for Excellence* includes an 'Early Level' (starting at three years old when children are in nursery and extending to the end of Primary 1) which is in principle play-based, as in mainland European countries. Sadly, its principles have not yet been translated into practice in the majority of P1 classes – or indeed in some nurseries. Our deeply embedded cultural expectation that four- and five-year-olds should be learning the three Rs is partly to blame – we've simply carried on doing what we always do. But these expectations have been exacerbated by media reports about educational policy in England and the USA where, over the last couple of decades, tests-and-targets educational regimes have led to a steady 'schoolification' of early years education. And it certainly hasn't helped that Scotland's 'Early Level' is split right down the middle: the first half takes place in nurseries (and is generally regarded merely as 'childcare') and the second in primary schools, so there is no feeling of coherence about the Early Level as a whole.

Then in autumn 2015, the First Minister – under pressure about Scotland's poverty-related attainment gap – announced the introduction of national assessment in literacy and numeracy, starting at Primary 1. Detailed targets for the age group were drawn up (known in Scotland as 'benchmarks') and the national standardised testing regime was introduced in the 2017-18 school year.

Ironically, as these political moves were going on, there was finally an upsurge of interest in turning the play-based principles of Early Level into practice in Primary 1 classes. It remains to be seen whether P1 teachers' enthusiasm for this project can weather the effects of the incoming national tests-and-targets regime. But in every other country where such a regime has taken hold, it has caused a narrowing of the curriculum, encouraged teachers to 'teach to the test' and steadily increased levels of anxiety about achievement among teachers, parents and pupils.

In these circumstances, learning through play is seldom prioritised over the teaching of literacy and numeracy skills in preparation for national tests, and it becomes increasingly difficult to provide a nurturing, relationship-centred 'kindergarten ethos'.

## Seen but not heard

The Scottish Government's decision to introduce national tests was based on the best of intentions. They were alarmed at the growing gap in educational attainment between children from low- and high-income families. So they naturally assumed that the best course of action was to focus attention on improving the three Rs, beginning – as seemed sensible to them – as soon as children start school. In making that assumption, however, they've inadvertently bolstered deeply-entrenched cultural attitudes about the care of young children, which are not consistent with current knowledge of child development.

They are, however, consistent with the robust Victorian values that led to our early school starting age in the first place. At a time when most adults believed 'children should be seen but not heard', it made absolute sense that infants should be herded into school the year they turned five and productively engaged in learning the three Rs. To hard-headed politicians in the 1860s, the joyful sound of children running, jumping, making dens and playing 'let's pretend' didn't seem remotely productive. But we now know that – if we are to avoid long-term, on-going costs in health, additional educational needs and social welfare provision – the sound of children at play is very important indeed. We also know that the under-sevens learn best through play, and their teachers support them best through forging positive, nurturing relationships.

By introducing a relationship-centred, play-based kindergarten stage, Scotland could ensure that all our children have the time, space and support to build firm foundations for formal education, while at the same time enhancing their potential for lifelong health and well-being. By ensuring that – as in the Nordic countries – a large proportion of every day's play takes place outdoors, we can return the sound of children playing to the heart of every community. And by maximising the use of local parks and green spaces, we can give the next generation the opportunity to learn and grow in the natural environment that's nourished the young of our species throughout history.

Our culture may be evolving at the speed of light these days, but biological evolution is a long, slow process. Young human beings still need what they have always needed for healthy development. In a culture that's increasingly urbanised, sedentary and screen-focused, we need a radical overhaul of universal care/education provision for the under-sevens to ensure they have frequent and regular opportunities to play, as often as possible outdoors and in nature.

We may not be able to bring the joyful sound of children playing back to all of Scotland's streets but by introducing a ring-fenced kindergarten stage we can ensure that our youngest citizens have the best possible chance of flourishing. &#9633;

---

This is an extended version of an article entitled *Samhchair nam Pàiste*, which appeared in the Gaelic magazine *Naidheachdan: AAA* in February 2018.

# Learning Outdoors: Healthy Challenges for All

Chalmers Smith

Chalmers Smith began his career as a teacher of Biology but has spent most of his working life in the realm of Outdoor Education. He has worked with all age groups in schools as well as training staff. He strongly believes all children and young people should have equal opportunities to learn outdoors. Although the outdoor education initiative he was part of in the 1970s never overtly set out to build confidence and resilience it was, in essence, precisely the educational journey on which it took young people. Chalmers spent eighteen months with Learning and Teaching Scotland (now Education Scotland) to develop learning outdoors within the Curriculum for Excellence.

I USE the term learning outdoors in this chapter as it focuses on the learner. However, the term equates to the more familiar term 'outdoor education'. I also use the term learning outdoors to include learning in school or centre grounds, outdoor adventure activities such as canoeing, skiing, rock climbing, camping and expeditions, residential visits to outdoor centres and expeditions abroad. My particular focus is on the 'formal' education sector where I strongly believe all children and young people should have equal opportunities to learn outdoors.

It is important to understand from the outset that learning outdoors is just one piece of a very, very large jigsaw in which educators and others are trying to help raise, amongst other aims, the confidence and resilience of young people. Examples include public speaking, playing a musical instrument, sport, taking part in a drama production, volunteering with other groups etc.

Research shows that in the late 1970s the formal provision of outdoor learning in the Edinburgh area was probably the most comprehensive in the world. I am proud to say that I was part of it. I changed from being a high school biology teacher to teach in the outdoors in the late 1970s. Being in a high school meant I was able to work with young people each year in a progressive and continuous way whilst trying to build confidence and resilience as part of their educational journey.

For example, during S2 and S3 we offered pupils a range of activities which they could undertake for four consecutive days. On day one of a kayaking course, young people would be challenged by getting in and out of a kayak safely, keeping balance, using a paddle for different strokes and getting wet and cold after a capsize. This flat-water day on a loch was followed by a trip on the Union Canal, a trip on the sea (weather permitting) and on the final day, a trip down part of the River Tweed. On this outing they had to use the skills they had acquired in previous days.

For me, the joy of watching confidence build in these young people was immeasurable. But for them (and their parents) there were tangible benefits from this immediate recognition of their achievements. We asked young people at the end of each course to evaluate their perceived progress: confidence, enjoyment, trying new activities and being 'in nature' all scored highly. At parents' nights, parents would often recall the impact of the experiences on their child and always in a positive and enthusiastic way.

Of course, one of the reasons why we were able to effectively challenge young people in this way is that we were also in the position to build relationships with them. Outdoor learning opportunities often involve long periods of talking and relationship building. Once on a coast walk with new S1 pupils we were chatting about the move from primary to high school. We were taken aback to learn that, despite doing a day 'taster' in June many still had a fear of starting high school. We then were able to introduce other ways of helping the transition.

**Outdoor learning in Scotland**

From my experience, lack of confidence and resilience in young people transcends all abilities and all socio-economic groupings. However, the opportunity to experience a range of outdoor learning situations is not equal as it is, largely, dictated by socio-economic factors and decisions taken at national, local authority and school level.

The difference good learning in the outdoors can make to pupils is what makes the erosion of opportunities in Scotland very difficult to accept. And there's no doubt that from the high point of the 1960s and 1970s, there has been a significant decline in outdoor learning. This decline took place from the 1980s to around the early 2000s. Research shows that during this period many local authority outdoor centres closed and provision in schools also declined.

From 2006 to around 2013 learning outdoors re-emerged as a key part of the new Curriculum for Excellence. As a consequence, Learning and Teaching Scotland (LTS) produced helpful guidance on outdoor learning. They also organised training opportunities in the outdoors for many teachers.

This revival of learning outdoors was short-lived as LTS was 'merged' with HM Inspectorate in 2011 to form a new body called Education Scotland. Priorities changed. Pressure on curricular changes increased and a focus on new exams meant that the focus on learning outdoors was downgraded. Funding streams were reduced and strategies redrawn.

Following the interest and resurgence of learning outdoors from 2006 onwards, research was undertaken to look at the amount of time children and young people in Scotland spent learning outdoors. It found that in the pre-school sector time spent outdoors as a proportion of the pre-school day increased from 23 per cent in 2006 to 36 per cent in 2014. Most of this was within the pre-school grounds.

In primary schools time spent outdoors had increased on average from 19 minutes per week in 2006 to 30 minutes per week in 2014. The locations for such outdoor learning included school grounds, beyond school grounds and residential trips. In secondary schools time spent outdoors increased on average from 13 minutes per week in 2006 to 16 minutes per week in 2014. Two thirds of this increase was spent on residential trips.

By contrast in Norway, a country with a similar size of population as Scotland, *Uteskole* (schools for 7 – 16 year olds) must, by law, provide learning outdoors for all students for one day per week or fortnight. This equates to between 150 to 300 minutes per week, a marked difference to Scotland's 16 to 30 minutes per week.

**Lack of central support**

The problem in Scotland is not just that there are not enough outdoor learning opportunities. There simply is not enough training or guidance. There is still a lot of fear about taking pupils out of school. Many staff members feel apprehensive when they hear the dreaded words 'risk assessment'. But they shouldn't. Despite the fact that outdoor learning is not a major priority in education, throughout the UK, millions of children and young people go on various outdoor trips throughout the year. These trips are considered safe and are encouraged by the Health and Safety Executive.

The situation is better than it was around ten years ago, when a strong risk-averse culture existed, but there is still room for improvement. The greater use of risk benefit assessment would be a good start as this makes people consider the benefits of an activity or situation on an equal basis to the risks. When I used this method with teachers, the benefits always outweighed the risks by two or even three to one. So, although risks exist and must, of course, be safely managed, the benefits to the young people are greater than the real or perceived risks. There is, however, no room for complacency and all training must be thorough and rigorous.

As staff are often expected to lead children and young people safely outdoors on a regular and progressive basis, it seems perfectly reasonable to expect that staff are given high quality training to manage groups in the outdoors. However, this is not the case.

The General Teaching Council for Scotland accepts outdoor learning as a subject and gives it professional recognition, yet trainee teachers are not required to do any formal training in learning outdoors whilst on graduate or post-graduate teacher training courses. This doesn't make sense: staff who are themselves confident in the outdoors will be better equipped to help instil confidence in young people whilst participating in these activities.

## Why learning outdoors matters

To my mind it's tragic that real opportunities in Scotland for quality outdoor learning have eroded at a time when pupils need its benefits more than ever. Young people are living in a world where stress is increasing. Exams, assessments and choosing subjects are all stressful. Technology is changing rapidly, and social media in all of its complex forms is to the fore. It is hardly surprising that research shows that the number of young people experiencing mental health issues is rising.

Learning in the outdoors could help improve young people's mental well-being. In the last few decades there has been a huge amount of research on the importance of what some call 'ecopsychology'. Some organisations now talk about 'green health' to communicate the importance of the natural world to human well-being. One early study showed that interaction with nature, even if it is only looking through a window at green spaces, helps to 'immunise' us by protecting us from future stress.

Research also shows the importance of physical activity not just to physical health but also mental health. The benefits of regular, physical exercise and participating in sports are well documented. Within a school context, most sports are, for very practical reasons, organised as team sports such as hockey and football. This works well for some young people but ignores the fact that many are neither 'team players' nor fond of competitive sports. They prefer to get involved in activities they can do on their own or with fewer people. Over the years I have witnessed many young people finding their 'niche' after they were introduced to activities such as cycling, orienteering, kayaking, rock climbing, sailing, skiing and mountaineering. Some pursue these activities for years after leaving school.

Leaving aside confidence and well-being, learning outdoors has other benefits. As the following three diverse examples drawn from my own experience illustrate, learning outdoors can have great transformative power in individuals' lives.

### A *defining moment*
On a four-day course in orienteering and archery for around 10 S2 pupils one of the girls in the group struggled academically in school. She also had poor physical coordination (at that stage undiagnosed) but was eager to try her best in both activities. Success was hard to come by but she persevered every day.

On day three whilst we were doing archery in the afternoon, we had moved back from the targets, from 10m to 15m. After a few minutes there was a huge 'whoop' as this girl had achieved the one and only bird's eye of the week with her second arrow. Her smile was wide and broad for many minutes and she looked like she had won a gold medal at the Olympics! Needless to say, her confidence rocketed and improved her later performances in the orienteering even though this requires a very different set of skills.

### *Winter camping*
We organised a joint camping trip between two schools for S2 pupils. The plan, after buying food and packing rucksacks etc., was for the groups to start at different places, walk towards

each other and camp for one night, leave the tents *in situ* and have a night together in a youth hostel before camping in the tents left on the third night.

All went well until the first night. . . around 02.00, the first group was subjected to gale force winds and heavy rain. During the night only one pupil tent survived and all 12 pupils had to huddle into it.

Morning brought a sorry scene as a bedraggled group tried to make breakfast and keep warm. It was mid-November and staff should have taken account of the weather and likely conditions during the planning phase.

Worse news was to come for the group, who had struggled with heavy rucksacks on the way in, with a promise of lighter rucksacks the following day. The wet and broken tents had to be dismantled and packed as they were of no use to the second group.

Initial dismay turned to acceptance and understanding and heavier rucksacks were duly packed. When we started walking to the youth hostel, not one person complained and a quiet first few minutes changed to chatter afterwards.

The resilience shown by every member of the group was exceptional and was talked about for many years to come.

*Pyrenees expedition*
We planned an expedition on a larger scale for a three-week trip to the Pyrenees. Plans started in August of the previous year with parents' nights and recruitment of pupils in S5 and S6. We organised weekends of training throughout the year to improve fitness and teach technical skills for moving on snow.

Travel to the Pyrenees was by minibus and took several days both ways. We camped at two locations in France and Spain and climbed several impressive peaks whilst undertaking some biology and geography fieldwork. We kept a journal and all members contributed to this by writing a daily diary.

The first contact, around three weeks after the trip, was from a mother of one of the girls who got in touch to say that her daughter's behaviour had changed dramatically. She was not only more confident and outgoing but also more willing to help around the house with different chores. When we finished the journal we held a final parents' night for group members. Again, parents talked about the positive differences they had noticed in their sons/daughters.

One entry from the journal about bivvying (sleeping in a sleeping bag outside on the ground with no tent) in the mountains was memorable. It simply stated: 'I never slept all night. It was the most horrible experience I've had.'

A full 18 years later, I received a Christmas card from a couple of people on the trip who had subsequently married and had taken up jobs in different parts of the world. One of them had written the message about their horrible experience. The message in the card read, 'Thank you for introducing us to many different activities in so many places, here and abroad, as it gave us the courage to *Carpe Diem* (seize the day).'

This tale chimes well with research undertaken in the late 1990s. It showed that adventures requiring a lot of effort and time have a larger impact on the learner than adventures involving narrower activities such as a zip wire descent.

There seems to be a general reluctance in Scotland (and

indeed the UK) to accept that some subject areas and inter-disciplinary topics are often better learned outdoors than indoors. Furthermore, it is remarkable, given the massive changes to society, culture, jobs and the whole world of information technology over the years, that the structure of our education system has hardly changed and is still similar to what was available a hundred years ago.

## A helpful comparison

This is not the case in other nations. In 2015 Finland was in the top five countries for reading and science and the top twelve for maths. As such, they were the envy of many nations.

However, between 2012 and 2016, Finland radically changed its education system to reflect modern life and living. Pupils, parents, teachers and local authorities were widely consulted in that order. Over 60,000 pupils responded to the consultation.

In the new system schools are still expected to teach subjects but they must devote more time on 'phenomenon' or topic teaching. This involves collaborative teaching with colleagues and aims to develop critical thinking in young people. Much of this takes place out of school but not always in the outdoors.

Finland provides other interesting statistics. Children start school at seven years old after a kindergarten year to develop cooperation and communication skills. There is no national testing. There are no league tables. Teachers are highly trained and qualified, are paid modestly and have much autonomy. Virtually all primary teachers have a Master's degree taken over three years. Only around 10 per cent of applicants for primary teacher posts are accepted. Schools are free from political 'interference'.

It would be naive and impractical to suggest lifting the educational system of one country into another but lessons can be learned from different countries on how education systems are evolving in modern times.

## A brighter future?

Recent developments in Scotland suggest there may be a change of thinking.

In 2016, The Care Inspectorate in Scotland produced a resource document for all pre-school establishments entitled 'My World Outdoors'. It states:

> Spending time outdoors and particularly in natural environments is good for all of us and especially for children. The Care Inspectorate recognises the benefits of accessing the great outdoors and this resource aims to make a positive contribution to the further development of outdoor play as part of early learning and childcare in Scotland.

By 2020 in Scotland the amount of free childcare will double from 15 to 30 hours per week and this has huge ramifications for all involved, not least in terms of accommodation and staffing. This may well result in more outdoor provision, including outdoor nurseries.

In 2017 Inspiring Scotland launched a year-long campaign for more play for children. The campaign had the full support of many key policy makers within major organisations in Scotland. The impact of this campaign will be of interest to many.

Another welcome development is the rapid rise of Upstart which is campaigning for a kindergarten stage in Scotland for children aged three to seven. Upstart stresses the importance of outdoor play. Upstart has only been going for a few years yet has an impressive number of supporters.

**Conclusion**

In the months and years to come, when politicians and policy makers make decisions on the future of our children and young people, the adults and citizens of tomorrow, I hope they take these decisions on the basis of robust evidence from around the world that outdoor learning can help children and young people learn and flourish.

If I had the ear of these politicians and policy makers I would suggest that they do the following:

1: Help children and young people in Scottish education improve their physical and mental well-being by ensuring that they have access to a series of quality, regular and frequent opportunities to learn in the outdoors.

2: Ensure that pre-service teachers in Scotland receive compulsory, comprehensive training on learning outdoors. This training should be undertaken by competent, knowledgeable and professional tutors. Practising teachers should also have access to regular updates and enhanced training opportunities in outdoor learning.

3: Enable more opportunities for children and young people to learn outdoors by ensuring schools and local authorities adopt the risk benefit assessment model and train all staff on its effective use.

4: Heed the evidence that broad adventure has a lasting effect on young people, and ensure that schools, in partnership with external agencies where necessary or appropriate, organise a series of planned, quality outdoor learning experiences which allow for 'broader adventure' activities.

5: Actively encourage schools to spend more quality time outdoors with children and young people, especially in subject areas and within topics which are best learned outdoors such as literacy, numeracy and health and well-being.

Finally, I would like to end with an inspiring quote from Tim Gill, an expert on young people and play. In his book *Nothing Ventured: Balancing risks and benefits in the outdoors*, he admirably sums up one of the main purposes of schools.

'Education in its broadest sense is not just about delivering a curriculum. It is about giving children the chance to extend their life skills. It is about developing their confidence. It is about fostering their resilience and sense of responsibility. And – let us not forget – it is about the enjoyment, engagement and excitement of venturing out into the real world, with all its capacity for uncertainty, surprise, stimulation and delight.' □

# The View from Room 13

Claire Newman

> Claire Newman is Chief Executive of Room 13 International
> and has worked with this highly creative initiative since she
> was introduced to it as a young woman studying art.
> Fifteen years on, her work with Room 13 has led her to travel
> extensively, presenting at some of Europe's most prestigious
> galleries and engaging with artists of all ages to help them set
> up their own Room 13 studios and projects. Her chapter
> vividly describes how Room 13 is an 'incubator of courage'
> for young people, building their confidence by providing an
> outlet for authentic self-expression.

THE FIRST Room 13 studio was set up in 1994 as an art studio
run by a group of children in Caol Primary School, near Fort
William. The view from the window of Room 13 hasn't changed
much, although a recent redevelopment of the school campus
means the studio has shifted approximately 20m southeast of
its original position. It's a panorama that takes in Ben Nevis
and views up the great glen to the east and north, and straight
down the loch towards Corran Ferry in the south.

This was the same view that inspired a group of children to
mount an expedition to 'see what's behind Ben Nevis'. Answer:
more mountains, as far as the eye can see. Later, the same group
attempted (after recruiting an adult support team) to walk all
the way across Scotland from their home village of Caol in the
West Highlands, to further satisfy their curiosity as to what lay
beyond. They failed in their attempt to reach the coast. A 5-day

walk covering 150 miles proved overly ambitious for a group of pre-teens. But lessons were learned. Important, possibly even life changing lessons. About nutrition and fitness and the benefits of planning. About personal limits, both physical and mental and what can be gained from pushing these. About perseverance, and perhaps what psychologists might call grit. But mainly, above all, about courage.

When the team realised they were going to fail in the stated aim of their expedition, they might have turned back and gone home, dejected. Instead, they were encouraged to reassess their situation. The expedition leader, a twelve-year-old P7 pupil called Mark, studied the map. Now that we know we're not going to be able to do what we planned, he asked of himself and the team, what can we do? From where we stand now, what is it possible for us to achieve? The team reset their objective, changed course and walked to the summit of Cairngorm. Then they called the school minibus, previously lined up to meet them at Stonehaven on the pre-arranged date and asked the driver to pick them up at Aviemore. They returned home satisfied with their achievement; resilient, even triumphant – possibly more so than if they had achieved their original objective.

I tell this story from a historical perspective. Although all of this took place when I was of a similar age to the participants, at that point I had not yet encountered the quiet anarchy of Room 13, where purposeful pre-teens are handed the ropes and encouraged to strive for outcomes that meet their own definition of success.

My own journey with Room 13 began with little more than the courage to make a phone call. After hearing about the Room 13 project via a family friend, I phoned up the artist in residence,

Rob Fairley, to learn more. I was encouraged to write a letter to the eleven-year-old Managing Director to volunteer my services as a 'studio assistant' on a programme of summer workshops that were planned.

Spending a summer volunteering in the Highlands, living on a croft and travelling 60 miles every day in the back of a pickup, to work in a creative studio where artists of all ages worked alongside each other with a shared sense of purpose and enquiry – this was my introduction to a whole new approach to life and art. My school-bound approach to art-making was turned upside down as I discovered in Room 13 an environment that was more creative and stimulating than anything I had encountered.

I grew up in Ayr, and from the age of 13 I travelled up and down to Glasgow School of Art to attend holiday courses, weekend workshops, evening classes, all of which I enjoyed enormously. However, with my introduction to Room 13 came the realisation that everything I was doing and learning in these classes was an extension of my high school art lessons. I thought I was in an adult environment, developing as an artist, when in fact I was completing a series of exercises and the results were entirely safe and predictable. This studio run by primary school pupils with their relentlessly questioning approach, exposed for me that the real roots of creative practice stem from original thinking. Not just demonstrating your skills and learning to handle the materials in the 'correct' way, but the searching and probing that comes with developing a sense of self. Your artwork, these children told me, has to *mean something*. This was new.

The following summer, I took the decision to forgo my application to art school and embark on what I anticipated would be an interesting gap year. A few weeks after leaving school, I took my bike and my backpack and boarded a train for Fort William. I took a part time job at the West Highland Museum and devoted the rest of my time to Room 13.

Fifteen years later my experiences with Room 13 have led me to travel extensively, undertake residencies and present work at some of Europe's most prestigious galleries and deliver training and lecturing at conferences and universities worldwide. I've set up and run a charitable organisation and stood up to make the case for its existence in boardrooms, classrooms and community halls. I've led groups of young people on expeditions overseas and residential summer schools for adults, worked with artists of all ages to help them set up their own Room 13 studios and projects and delivered art projects and commissions myself in collaboration with young artists and whole communities. I never did make it to art school. I own a flat in Fort William and a newer, shinier bicycle. I still don't know if my artwork means anything, but my work in the broader sense encompasses a greater sense of purpose than my teenage self could have imagined.

I still wonder how as a 17-year-old I had the courage to embark on all of this. Talking with some young adults who grew up with Room 13 has led me to reflect on Room 13's role as an incubator of courage. Sharing their experiences of Room 13, these individuals overwhelmingly speak of a time and space in their lives where they were supported to think and to explore, to strive and try, and the ways in which this has served them in adulthood.

Sammy Stuart grew up with Room 13 in Primary School. He is now 18 years old and living in Dundee, where he has just finished an acting and performance course and is now embarking on a career in sociology. As a teenager, Sammy Stuart took the decision to identify as a male and is an activist for LGBT+ rights.

Sammy remembers Room 13 as 'a safe place that was also really expressive':

> As a kid you are always trying to tell people what you are thinking, but [often] it doesn't really work. At the time I remember thinking I'm happiest when I'm here, and I can speak most when I'm here. I didn't really have a concept of building confidence over an extended period of time when I was a kid, but I did know that I could speak and be heard and feel like I had something to say in Room 13.

Sammy reckons his job as Treasurer of Room 13 built in him an awareness of consequences, which he believes is key to building and sustaining confidence as you get older and become more aware of the consequences of your actions and decisions. 'I'd say I had more courage now, even though as a kid I would speak up more; at the moment I speak up for things that are more sensitive and will face more backlash.'

He feels there are many reasons young people may be lacking in courage:

> From the age of five you're sat down and you're given tests and you get big red Xs and frowny faces on all your stuff. But if you leave an answer blank, then you don't get any reaction. I think that instils the idea in kids that doing nothing will create no effect and doing something might create a bad effect. So it creates a lot of anxiety and, as you grow up, that doesn't change really. Because if you try stuff and then fail at it, you're opening yourself up to mockery and general discontent. Whereas if you don't try at all

you are less likely to face that. So that's linked to
courage. Without getting help to build the courage,
to try, even though you might fail, just try it anyway,
then you're left with a whole bunch of anxious
youngsters who just want to pass their exams.

Sammy Stuart believes taking pride in yourself and your work is the way to combat this inherent anxiety. 'You've just got to do a whole lot of thinking and making and make stuff that makes you proud that you made it. Pride and courage sort of come together. Having pride helps you have courage because if you believe that you can achieve stuff, you can actually come out better that if you had not done something scary.'

Ruaridh, a self-confessed 'young tearaway' turned poet, is a guy who knows what it is to do something scary. When he stood up to recite his work in front of an audience of his teachers and peers, he was exposing a part of himself that been kept deeply hidden behind a cultivated persona of bravado and disruptive behaviour.

I was at that age where I thought I was a big macho
guy and thought no-one had to know that this person
had feelings. When it came down to art, I thought I
was the most useless person ever so I was really,
really wary and didn't really think I'd enjoy it.

It took a bit of progression to realise that it wasn't
just that sort of thing that made someone good at art.
Art was more of a collective thing. In Room 13, we
did haiku poems and the realisation that art in itself
wasn't just finger painting and drawing was quite a
big thing for me. I was quite intrigued with writing;
how I felt, putting it into poems. In my head, no one
would know that was about me. So it was conveying
my own thoughts and feelings in a way I felt safer
doing it.

Initially, Ruaridh refused to engage with the Room 13 project at the local youth centre. He tried to disrupt the workshops, mocking the artists and other kids taking part with foul mouthed insults. The artists leading the project persevered, and after a few weeks Ruaridh began to open up. He embraced poetry and went on to recite his work at the Youth Scotland annual conference and at the Scottish Parliament.

> [Before,] I had confidence but not in the right way. I
> had the confidence to shout out the stupid remark or
> to get in your face and stuff like that. I didn't really
> have the confidence to stand up and talk to people, if
> it was a serious matter. I didn't have the confidence
> to talk about my personal self. I had the confidence in
> a wrong way.

Ruaridh is in no doubt about the significance of this experience in shaping his journey into adulthood:

> Going through high school, before I was in Room 13,
> I was getting suspended most weeks. I was getting in
> fights, I was getting in trouble. From when I started
> to when I finished Room 13 I was never suspended.
> I was never kicked out of school. I graduated and I
> got Highers and went to College. Now I'm doing a
> job I love. Now, I've got the confidence on a daily
> basis. I stand up and talk to people about serious
> matters almost every single day.
>
> I would honestly say that had it not been for going
> into Room 13, I reckon I wouldn't have changed at
> all. My personality has changed since then because
> when I first started I just wasn't a nice person to be
> around. I was quite an angry person. I'm a lot calmer
> now and I think about things more clearly.

Both Sammy Stuart and Ruaridh link the growth of courage and confidence to finding an outlet for authentic self-expression.

For them, as for me, the realisation that art should mean something provided a turning point.

This was also true for Ciara, a young person suffering in silence. Ciara experienced bullying in high school and suffered the effect of this throughout her teenage years. As a participant in a Room 13 project she created the powerfully emotive artwork: It Won't Be Like This Forever.*

> I think it's easy for young people to get confidence and courage mixed up and that can have really negative consequences. Those who are not confident might not think that speaking out about their own experiences is brave or courageous when in fact it is. I used to feel really ashamed to even use the word bullying to describe my experience because the people who did bully me would laugh at the thought of describing what they were doing as that and so would the onlookers. But, having been given the platform to openly talk about and create something [informed by] my own experience, I had the chance to show courage in another light. The work allowed me to reflect on myself and express this honestly in a way that benefited me and others.

Ciara is now in her twenties, and recently graduated from Edinburgh University with a law degree. She also tells us:

> I think the answer for showing courage is talking

---

* 'It Won't Be Like This Forever' Ciara McCartney 2012.
An old-style school desk with a lid that lifts open. On the outside surface of the desk the artist has carved and scrawled the names and comments that she would be bombarded with every day at school by her tormentors; 'Slut', 'UGLY', 'Skinny bitch' etc. Open up the desk and the interior is painted matt black. The artist has rigged up fairy lights and on the reverse of the desk lid, she has painted glittery stars and the words 'It Won't Be Like This Forever'.

about whatever is going on in your own life and feeling like it's ok to do so. That in itself is courageous, as we know sometimes people get to the point that lack of talking results in horrible consequences, so I think it is important that young people are given a platform to speak openly and honestly about whatever is on their minds.

One thing Sammy Stuart, Ruaridh and Ciara agree on is that they were lucky. They happened to have Room 13 in their lives, or stumble across it much as I did. Having such an environment is not a given for the majority of young people growing up in Scotland.

As Ruaridh notes:

I stumbled across Room 13 and obviously it had such a dramatic effect on me positively. I know from working with kids in Glasgow that that isn't always an option for people. Some people don't have that stumbling thing that provides a turning point for them. They stay the way I was. They stay angry, they stay confused. They don't find that thing that helps them. There isn't a Room 13 out there for everyone, if you know what I mean.

Indeed while Room 13 originated in Scotland there are more projects in Nepal or in Africa than there are here. There has been *ad hoc* development of new studios and interest from schools and communities in Highland, and also in the south of Scotland, but no structured approach to support this. For our part this is due not to lack of interest but lack of resources.

There is, as yet, no formal process for 'registering' a Room 13 studio. There is a degree of fluctuation as new studios and projects come and go. Not all studios resemble each other closely in terms of the way they function – e.g. a full time dedicated studio with an artist in residence in a paid position vs one afternoon a week pop-up project run by volunteers – so these variations make it difficult to count and measure the different Room 13s.

We can be confident that Room 13 has been adopted in some form by schools or communities in 15 countries, and we have over 40 active contacts worldwide (though one individual may offer a point of contact for several studios or projects).

Each Room 13 studio offers a space where young artists can work alongside a professional adult artist in residence and are encouraged to be creative and to think for themselves.

Room 13 studios strive to embrace the global with the local, providing access to arts, creativity and culture in an environment that supports dialogue and debate, critical thinking, risk and experimentation to inform the production of thoughtful, inspiring, high quality work.

Reflecting on what has changed for us as a result of our experiences in Room 13 invites consideration on what needs to change for young people so they may more commonly access opportunities for authentic self-expression and to develop that sense of purpose.

> 'Role models and people around you can push you on a little bit and help you along, but courage is something that comes from yourself, it's not something that you can teach.'

Among the young adults I spoke to, having a role model, or a champion, seemed to be a key factor in developing courage as was having a goal or a greater purpose. Returning to the story at the opening of this chapter bears this out.

The story of the Room 13 trans-Scotland expedition team didn't end with their trek to the summit of Cairngorm. For three of the boys who took the lead on that particular expedition, the experience nurtured a greater ambition. A few years later the boys, bigger, stronger and approaching their 16th birthdays, set their sights on Mount Everest. However, one thing they had learned from their previous failed attempt was to scale their ambitions. So when they set out to walk from Kathmandu to the Everest region, it was not the summit they were aiming for but base camp.

The journey to having confidence is not a singular achievement. Through a series of ups and downs, we are at all times aiming for our own personal base camp. A safe, expressive place from which we can venture out into the world to make attempts on our goals, or to which we can retreat when we have pushed too far. □

# Whitdale Primary School: Resilience and *Bounce Back!*

Iain McDermott

> Iain McDermott is headteacher of Whitdale Primary School in West Lothian. It is a large two stream school built fifty years ago, with attached early years centre, serving a mixed catchment within a busy, community driven town. The current roll is just shy of 400 structured across fifteen classes. Iain came to the post in January 2014. Being new to the school helped both him and the new deputy head to take an objective viewpoint and see what was required to take the school even further forward.
>
> Their vision is to create a safe and happy community, and a curriculum which inspires, engages, challenges and enables learning that lasts a lifetime. The school has a strong commitment to ensuring excellence and equity for all pupils and staff believe that everyone has the capacity to realise their full potential and to flourish.

WHEN TAKING on a new headteacher role in a school, it is important to evaluate and assess existing cultures, habits, practices and how they shape the values of all stakeholders. I firmly believe that before any impact can be made on raising attainment and achievement, school leaders need to understand the learning community for which they are now responsible. If we genuinely believe that all stakeholders can have a positive effect on our children, it is vital to listen to as many people as possible before coming up with ideas on how to improve the school's activities and culture. Therefore, in the first six months in my new post, I took the opportunity to engage the whole school community – staff, parents and pupils – in establishing exactly what everyone saw as the values and visions for Whitdale Primary School.

During a discussion with the school's educational psychologist, the name of Professor Martin Seligman from the University of Pennsylvania was brought up. He is a leading authority on positive psychology and resilience, and a recognised expert on interventions that build strengths and well-being. His latest book *Flourish* was recommended as a valuable resource to explore his five pillars of positive psychology: Positive Emotion, Engagement, Relationships, Meaning and Accomplishment (PERMA, for short). We then set about framing staff sessions around the principles of Martin Seligman's work. Initial activities for staff included reading sections of *Flourish* and completing 'the Values In Action (VIA) Survey of Character Strengths'.

It would be fair to say that both of these tasks took some staff members out of their comfort zones. Exploring concepts of happiness and personal well-being through academic reading and carrying out a 240-question survey challenged perceptions. Some staff members were apprehensive about revealing aspects of their personality and character. However, initial trepidation subsided and through careful planning, time allocation and a welcoming supply of tea and biscuits, we saw our first authentic engagement from staff. The questionnaire results highlighted key strengths across our school community. With our educational psychologist, staff explored similarities, difference, ways to build on these and even produced wonderfully varied and artistic shields (still proudly hanging in the staffroom) to personally visualise our collective character strengths.

Upper primary pupils (Key Stage 2) also undertook a child friendly 'VIA Survey of Character Strengths' to provide a baseline audit of our pupils and to enable teachers to explore themes of happiness and well-being within the classroom. Both of these questionnaires were crucial to establishing an understanding of positive psychology and I would recommend both highly.

### Adopting a 'solution-oriented approach'

Our second aim was to engage staff in professional learning around 'solution-oriented approaches'. This tool, developed over the past three decades by a number of leading psychologists, focuses on 'what works' in any given situation and the development of detailed descriptions of goals. In developing and expanding these descriptions, new possibilities for change open up both for the individual and the organisation.

As a school leader, it was important for me to ensure that our work in developing an understanding of positive psychology would also have a tangible impact on well-being, learning and pupil development. In order to do this, we connected themes from Seligman's *PERMA* pillars of positive psychology with solution-oriented practice that helps people develop goals and solutions rather than explore and analyse current problems.

The solution-oriented principles that school staff strived to embed – slowly and appropriately – were based on Bernadette Cairns and Michael Harker's paper 'Empowering Change' which was published by the Scottish Government in 2008. This provided meaningful, effective guidance and became a focal point for valuable professional learning led by our link educational psychologist. It also provided the basis for ongoing development of restorative approaches for the whole school community. This guidance can be summarised as follows:

- Listen to the person, listen for the possibility

- People have the necessary resources to make changes

- Everyone has their own ways of solving problems

- Collaboration enhances change

- Language shapes and moulds how we make sense of the world

- A focus on future possibilities and solutions enhances change

- There are always exceptions to the problem

- Small changes can lead to bigger change

- If it works do more of it; if it doesn't do something different

- The problem is the problem, not the person.

The third part of our initial process was to ensure that the time taken in developing staff understanding of positive psychology, including character strengths, was reflected in an agreed set of values, the schools related policies and crucially our curriculum rationale. Everyone involved so far felt that it was important that visitors to our school could *see, feel and hear* a culture that valued each other's strengths and benefitted from everyone's commitment to work together.

With this in mind I, and the school leadership team, set up a variety of engagement opportunities with parents, pupils and partners. These included focus group discussions, online surveys, and that good old-fashioned tactic of 'catching' people at events (often by enthusiastic pupil representatives!). Engaging stakeholders who are often busy or focused on different agendas remains a challenge for all schools. Time is precious for everyone, so with this in mind we kept our audit lens clearly and simply focused on one simple question: *'What do we want for our children at our school?'*

All responses were warmly welcomed, varied, always interesting and included what we would have hoped for. Parents wanted to have their children valued as individuals, for teachers to know their pupils well and tailor support as necessary. Pupils wanted learning to be fun, and for their school to be a safe environment. Partners wanted to be included in the life of the school and for them to be considered as valuable contributors across our community.

Once collated this audit process evidence was invaluable in helping us construct a values-based rationale for our school that all stakeholders agreed on. We all wanted to develop a learning community that would *inspire, engage, challenge and flourish.*

**Theory into practice**

As a result of the exploration of the concepts of positive psychology, it became apparent that in order to make things happen we needed to turn theory into practice. Working with our educational psychologist we explored the principles of solution-oriented approaches to provide the foundation to build sustainable, restorative school practices that could be applied at all levels across our learning community. The key things that we wanted to achieve were to:

- Increase pupil motivation

- Enhance pupil self-management (e.g. anger, anxiety)

- Tackle bullying behaviour and improve relationships

- Support learning and teaching

- Provide peer support for teachers and pupils

- Facilitate effective multi-agency working

- Enhance school self-evaluation and development

Throughout my time as headteacher, the school has been committed towards the principles of nurture. West Lothian Council has shown a strong belief and commitment in developing nurture groups in schools for a number of years through professional learning and considerable finance, something that has greatly benefitted pupils across the authority. These principles have helped formulate the school's restorative support approaches such as cooperative learning, and staged assessment and intervention.

All classes from nursery to P7 develop a shared class charter, based around clear principles of positive psychology. This is written in child friendly language that describes the types of behaviours one would hope to see, hear and feel within that learning environment. These are creatively displayed in classrooms and signed by all involved in creating it. The charters allow teachers and pupils to engage in meaningful discussion around positive behaviour choices, restorative support for when things don't always go to plan and the benefits for everyone in following them. Over the years, pupils and parents have positively commented about the value of the charter process and having them as 'their own'.

Staged assessment and interventions begin at the start of the first level in Curriculum for Excellence (P.2). Pupils who may require further support, as identified through observation and assessment, engage in structured nurture groups. These focus on the development of social skills through activities, games, tasks and a lot of positive reinforcement from specifically trained teachers and support workers. These groups closely follow the principles and practices of nurture as successfully established through the school's links with the Nurture Group Network. They have been incredibly valuable in developing resilience and social aptitude in younger children. The social aspect of a small group allows a safe, secure environment for these pupils. Our structured formative and summative assessments tools (such as the Boxall profile) have provided clear substantial evidence that such approaches incorporating nurture, positive psychology and resilience help children to socially interact more successfully. They also allow them to access learning more readily and are a clear factor in raising attainment.

As the pupils progress through our school, targeted intervention remains a focus to ensure that all pupils receive the most appropriate, equitable support for their well-being. A flexible, responsive planning model allows us to establish short life support groups as and when required. These provide restorative social skill development for those children that require encouragement and nurture. Sometimes these have taken the form of small group work or one to one sessions – lasting several weeks or several days depending on need. Again, crucial to the success of these interventions has been the school's commitment to provide training and professional learning for all staff. Rather than seeing this as a challenge, we strive to ensure that a commitment to professional learning is a priority for all and that as a school leadership team we promote and support this. This continues to be a vital part of the yearly planning for the school leadership team. It ensures that the latest and best theories of learning are made available to ensure consistency for all our children.

Like any learning community, behaviour issues come and go, and no school leader can truly say that they have eradicated completely the factors that hinder a harmonious environment. However, comments and feedback from parents continue to be positive and it is always great to have recognition for the work the school undertakes to build positive relationships and resilience. Regular 'drop in' opportunities for nurture group parents provide valuable time for sharing strategies and involving families in what their children are engaging in and celebrating success. Parents and carers have also commented through questionnaires and meetings on how welcoming the school is, how positive the ethos and the impact the whole school approaches are having on pupil resilience. 'It's like a small school feeling in a big school', was one parent's comment.

Pupil feedback is also very good. This can be seen in our most recent standardised assessment attitudes scores at P.4 and P.7. This shows that 94 per cent of pupils enjoy or really enjoy their time at school. Similarly, pupil focus groups' comments positively highlight the 'way that everyone helps you and makes you feel good about yourself'.

### *Bounce Back!*

In the autumn of 2015, eighteen months after I took up the post of headteacher at Whitdale Primary School, we took the decision to further support our well-being agenda by introducing the Australian resiliency programme *Bounce Back!* It is a resource which has been extensively used and rightly lauded within Australian education. For almost a year we considered whether it would be a valuable tool for resilience building and developing skills in resourcefulness for our pupils. I was encouraged by a quote by one of its authors, Dr. Toni Noble. In an article describing *Bounce Back!* she stated:

> We can't protect young people from the stress of all potential adverse life events but we, as educators, can make a significant contribution to their welfare and lifelong learning by teaching them coping skills and creating the class and school environments that promote their resilience.

As with all school improvement initiatives, staff always welcome an injection of inspiration; a spark to reignite creativity or a flexible framework that can provide support for existing learning. On reflection, *Bounce Back!* did this for us. Importantly, and in keeping with our principles of transparency and inclusive engagement with all staff, we set aside substantial time from our professional learning calendar ahead of the introduction of the programme. This collegiate learning was facilitated in association with Morag Kerr from the Centre for Confidence and Well-being. She provided engaging, relevant and thought-provoking input that enabled staff to discuss well-being and see where our journey was taking us. It also allowed time for staff to view the associated *Bounce Back!* materials and stimulate ideas for framing learning about resilience within our school's culture and context.

Two years down the line, members of the staff team have fond memories of the session and the introduction of *Bounce Back!*

into our school. It came at a vital time as the school was beginning to triangulate existing work on well-being. This input gave us time for critical reflection on the impact we were making in building resilience in our pupils. I was really pleased to hear how impressed our *Bounce Back!* trainer was with the attitude that our staff had on the day we worked together. When asked what they did to cheer themselves up on a bad day their response was, 'Well we don't really have bad days, things just happen and you get on with it.' This was a response Morag Kerr had not heard anywhere else when delivering *Bounce Back!* training.

Following the positive staff training day and familiarisation with the resources, groups of teachers took the opportunity to embed and match up the resource units and outcomes with the school's existing health and well-being pathways. Across the school, teachers have developed a variety of different ways of incorporating *Bounce Back!* into their classrooms. This allowed staff the flexibility to use the resource as and when it could have the biggest impact with pupils.

In the early years classes, stories and literature provide the focus for engaging pupils in themes relevant to resilience and risk taking. Story books and nursery rhymes such as *The Three Little Pigs* also allow teachers to create play opportunities for children to explore these themes and for the teachers to engage in or observe responses.

Teachers in 1st level classrooms (P.2-4) have used drama and literacy as useful vehicles to explore resilience with pupils. Again, building on narrative based contexts, stories such as *Matilda* by Roald Dahl open up rich contexts for children to role play safely and learn about aspects of loss, change, separation and resilience. Teachers have also looked to develop interdisciplinary contexts for the themes in *Bounce Back!* Most notable here is through the development of outdoor learning. Again this offers a safe structured environment for children to explore themes. Simple playground games such as group skipping or even elimination games such as *duck, duck, goose* can allow teachers and pupils to consider what resilience looks like.

Towards the latter years of the primary, teachers have used social studies contexts to develop the themes of *Bounce Back!* In one memorable project one P.7 teacher took themes of World War Two evacuees, as described in *Carrie's War* by Nina Bawden, and asked pupils to create drama *tableaux* and write poetry exploring loss and separation. In this case, a historical topic facilitated a contextual space for pupils to safely identify feelings that, despite being over sixty years old, could be easily identified – and empathised with – by a P.7 class in 2017.

As *Bounce Back!* developed across the curriculum, we also saw the value of developing themes from the programme with parents and carers. Parental workshops, initially in our nursery class, took place to enable staff to share the importance of building resilience at home. These led onto the development of our established 'Stay, Play and Learn' nursery sessions. Here parents joined their children and had a first-hand opportunity to experience learning contexts where structured risk taking could take place – both inside and outside. More importantly they were able to observe ways the staff responded to children making mistakes or trying things unfamiliar to them. In other words, where failure and trying again were parts of everyday learning. Similar opportunities to share the messages of *Bounce Back!* and resilience were embedded into whole school parental learning events, assemblies, workshops and presentations – often led by pupils. Responses from parents were always positive. They often said that they welcomed strategies from *Bounce Back!* for developing their own approaches at home.

Equally important was involving support staff in professional learning and discussion on how *Bounce Back!* can benefit our playground environment. This work at Whitdale, whilst still ongoing, is providing us with the opportunity to develop playtimes that are more focused on developing resilience. Support staff now have a better understanding of their role in facilitating and enabling an environment of structured risk taking. We also now have a fully developed peer mentoring system in operation, with trained P.7 pupils on hand to assist with disagreements or disputes through the offer of restorative discussions at designated 'buddy stops'.

Since our initial training in 2015, *Bounce Back!* continues to be a cornerstone of the school's health and well-being curriculum being used with whole classes throughout the year. It is also at the core of work with small groups requiring additional support and also one to one targeted support. Feedback from pupils has been overwhelmingly positive and there are clear indications of its impact on improved pupil behaviour, and the number of significant incidents and exclusions.

Assessment data also indicates that investing time in building resilience can be a contributory factor to pupils' attainment, progress and achievements. The last two years have seen a steady increase in the number of pupils achieving expected Curriculum for Excellence levels at key transition stages. May 2017 data show that 11 per cent more pupils achieving reading at P.1 (reception year), 16 per cent more achieving numeracy at P.4 (year 3) and 11 per cent more pupils achieving writing at P.7 (year 6) than in

August 2016. Notably, a considerable proportion of these increases have been seen in pupil groups who have benefitted from additional support both academically and within social support groups.

At Whitdale Primary School, we see *Bounce Back!* as a vital resource that assists us to build resilience and exemplify the values we believe in as our pupils grow and develop. We also hope to involve parents and carers more actively in understanding the value of resilience building through focused group work. We also passionately believe that this work can improve attainment and provide support for those families across our community for whom poverty is a daily reality. □

# Transforming Trajectories: Confidence and Resilience-building in Big Noise, Raploch

Kathryn Jourdan

Kathryn Jourdan is a member of the Board of Sistema Scotland as well as being a viola player, teacher and researcher. Sistema Scotland is a charity with the goal of creating permanent social change in some of the most deprived communities in Scotland through the Big Noise orchestra programmes. It aims to change lives by fostering confidence, discipline, teamwork, pride and aspiration in the children and young people taking part. Kathryn's chapter describes the work of Sistema Scotland and, through the voices of young members of the orchestra, the life-changing impact this has had on individuals and communities.

SISTEMA Scotland is a charity established in 2008 which seeks to enable long term social transformation in communities which have faced profound challenges over recent decades, through the delivery of a high quality, immersive and inclusive music education and social programme. Sistema Scotland uses the model of the orchestra as a vehicle for effecting change, inspired by the *El Sistema* music education programme in Venezuela.

> The inclusive nature of the orchestra, its capacity to include large numbers of children of different ages and stages, its flexibility in delivering diverse methods of learning and its potential for promoting healthy social pedagogy, make it an ideal medium through which children can develop confidence, teamwork, resilience, problem solving skills, pride and aspiration, as well as the capacity to work hard; all of

which will support them to reach their potential and lead successful and fulfilled lives. This is a multi-faceted, long-term intervention supporting the children to work together for a common goal and the pursuit of excellence in music through a pathway of involvement from birth to adulthood.

(Self-evaluation report submitted for Education
Scotland's inspection, April 2017)

There are currently four Big Noise centres – in Raploch Stirling, Govanhill in Glasgow and the Torry community in Aberdeen, with a programme in Douglas, Dundee having launched very recently. Each programme is shaped in response to the needs of the local community, but there are common threads of delivery which run throughout each centre. The discussion here will focus on Big Noise Raploch, the first centre to be established in Scotland, based in the community campus which houses Raploch's three primary schools. Now in its tenth year, the first young people to become involved are beginning to leave school, and narratives are emerging of the effects that Big Noise has had upon these longer established members of the programme.

This chapter seeks to give a voice to some of these young people as they reflect upon their experiences at Big Noise, and how the music-making-within-relationship which characterises the programme has shaped their lives so far.

## Big Noise programme: immersive and inclusive

The programme starts with Baby Noise, a group for parents and carers of babies and toddlers, where Big Noise staff lead early music-making sessions. This continues through nursery classes and pre-instrumental 'musicianship' curriculum provision for P1s and P2s. Pupils of Raploch Primary, Our Lady's and Castleview schools are all involved at this stage. New technology, specially adapted instruments and notation facilitates the learning of those with profound additional needs at Castleview and involves all the children at the school.

By the end of P2 pupils choose a stringed instrument, learning in groups and, from the outset, play in an emerging orchestra. At P3 afterschool sessions begin, building to four days a week and during holiday periods. Where appropriate these provide healthy snacks, breakfast and lunch. Several orchestras of different age groups and levels ensure a progression of learning for the young musicians. We use a whole range of styles of music and Big Noise staff bring expertise in a huge variety of approaches to music education, community music-making and performance.

At P5 we offer woodwind, brass and percussion instruments, giving further opportunities for those who might prefer to play one of these. As young people make the transition to high school they continue to attend the afterschool sessions and holiday weeks, with the involvement of Big Noise staff in some of their High School music-making. We invite adult members of the community to learn an instrument in the context of The Noise orchestra. This attracts a mix of parents, carers, and grandparents from Raploch, teachers from the Raploch schools and volunteers from Big Noise. Not only is Big Noise open to every child living in Raploch, but staff are also committed to repeatedly offering opportunities to become involved. They go to extraordinary lengths to make sure that any challenging behaviour is dealt with positively, with young people always given another chance to participate. Young musicians from the wider Stirling area are invited to join some of the holiday weeks.

Committed to an inclusive and immersive experience of music-making, Big Noise staff also practise a pedagogical pluralism, where no one methodology holds sway. Amongst the staff of musicians are practitioners from all over the world and they bring expertise from Kodaly, Colour Strings, Carl Orff, Dalcroze, Paul Rolland and Suzuki methods, amongst others.

The team works on the basis that musical excellence goes hand in hand with social transformation: that high aspirations and excellence in teaching are key to bringing about change. In order to effect the generational change to which Sistema Scotland aspires it is essential for us to establish a permanent presence in the Big Noise communities.

## The orchestra as a model for social transformation

José Antonio Abreu founded Venezuela's *El Sistema* programme more than 40 years ago when he began rehearsing an orchestra of young people. Gradually he widened participation to include many *nucleos* or centres across the country, developing an orientation towards social transformation; giving opportunities to young people to become immersed in music-making as a means of changing life trajectories and diverting young people away from negative outcomes associated in the Venezuelan context with misuse of drugs and crime.

Richard Holloway, a well-known public figure in Scotland, visited Venezuela in 2006, returning inspired to set up a music education programme in Scotland. Like Abreu he hoped this might address some of the intractable issues he saw across the country. Holloway thought it could offer a hopeful and absorbing alternative to youngsters living in communities which felt marginalised and alienated and which had suffered from rapid post-industrial social and economic change.

But why was Holloway so attracted to the idea of music-making and the orchestra in particular? First because it is a social activity where healthy relationships are formed musically and socially. It provides an opportunity for individuals to thrive within a community. What's more it encourages personal agency: members of the community are empowered to bring about change in their own lives and to transform their community through participating in music-making together. Unlike other programmes based on sporting models, for example, the orchestra allows a professional to play to the best of their ability alongside a virtual beginner. This is because any piece of music lends itself to adaptation for a spectrum of simple to much more complex lines. This side-by-side model of rehearsal and perform-ance is a central practice of Big Noise programmes, allowing partnership with professional orchestras in Scotland, such as the BBC Scottish Symphony Orchestra and, in the recent past, the Simón Bolívar Symphony Orchestra of Venezuela.

This brief sketch of the structures and vision of Big Noise programmes, and Big Noise Raploch in particular, sets the scene for an exploration of how the practices of music-making through relationship affect young people themselves. What follows is a summary of semi-structured interviews with six young people who have participated in the Big Noise community since its very beginning and for whom music-making in this community has provided opportunities which have changed their lives. I have used pseudonyms to preserve the young people's anonymity.

**Building confidence and resilience through music-making**

The first topic to arise in many of the interviews concerned the social and emotional skills which the young musicians felt they had developed through the support of Big Noise staff members, as they participated in learning their instrument and playing in the various levels of orchestra alongside their peers. Sam described how she wouldn't talk to anyone as a young primary pupil, finding it extremely hard to relate to others:

> Big Noise came along and they did team exercises to get you talking to people. You did singing games – just bringing out your confidence. I wouldn't want to talk, but then there would be singing and I quite liked it. So I sang, and we got to know quite a bit about each other first, so it was good. That made me feel more confident, and I made friends within Big Noise, and now I'm in high school and I've got quite a few friends, and if I didn't have this, then I wouldn't be the person I am today. The staff will come alongside you and help you through whatever you need. Basically we're one big family. Everyone's here for each other – young people as well as the staff.

Sam describes the transition from primary to secondary school as presenting a fresh challenge in terms of getting to know a new set of people: 'But there was the fact that if I could make friends when I was a young girl, I can do it now. . . I still find it hard today, but it's just who I am.'

Her hard-won confidence had developed into resilience, as she drew upon her past experience of working through difficulties to develop new social skills.

Amy told me of how over the past few years Big Noise staff members encouraged her to represent the organisation at public events. She is now a highly effective, compelling communicator, as I witnessed when she presented to the Sistema Scotland Board recently. She told me:

> Big Noise has given me the confidence to do quite a lot of the stuff I'm doing now. So if I hadn't done all the speeches that I've done for Big Noise, for the Board and that, and giving the concerts, I would never have been able to go into an interview. Even when I was twelve there's no way I would stand in front of a classroom even of my own pals and say anything. I had a stutter. As soon as we started doing concerts I realised that if I had just played my instrument to 8000 people (in the Big Concert) how could I not talk to my class? I can do this, and if I don't do it I'm not going to get anything out of it. I realised that Big Noise was helping me do other things than the music. Because I didn't want to do music [as a career], but I enjoyed playing for the recreation, for the fun.

Joe described his younger self as 'a troubled child' and particularly appreciates the patience and perseverance shown by staff:

> When I actually started Big Noise, through primary school I was taught that I was stupid and dumb and all that stuff, and lazy. . . just because I was dyslexic. And we never knew until I got to high school. Throughout that time I was angry, upset. I was just a real pain to deal with. I would scream, shout, run away. . . do all that stuff, but Big Noise never gave up on me, and I got to fourth year and started to realise, 'What am I doing?' Big Noise has really helped me build more confidence and see that I am better than I really was. When I would throw a tantrum they wouldn't take offence, or shout at me. They would just wait until I had calmed down, then they would talk and ask what was wrong. Just really being that support. I think there's a lot of children in Raploch who need that support.

For Louise the sense of solidarity amongst Big Noise young musicians had been even more significant than the support of staff in helping her overcome situations where she was being bullied at primary school: 'Everyone started sticking up for me because they got to know me better,' she recounted.

Johnathon talked to me of the sectarianism which can linger in the wider community. At Big Noise, he said, the staff have created an environment free from this, which gives him the confidence to feel good about his identity as a Catholic.

Music and participation in the orchestra also boosted the young people's confidence and resilience. Joe recalled how learning to read music was tricky for him, but with Big Noise staff helping him he realised he was able to learn, and found it was fun: 'But then I'd get stuck, and my confidence would drop,' he says. 'Then Big Noise staff would say, 'It's all right – do it this way!' It was easier, and my confidence would bounce right back.'

Taylor told me of how she used to get so nervous before exams at school that she would cry. But her experience at Big Noise has helped her cope with this. The staff discovered that she has a lovely voice, and encouraged her to use it, so every year now she sings a solo in the summer-school concert. She observed: 'I start off the song really nervous, but as I get into the song I become more confident because I realise I'm doing all right.' Furthermore, she feels singing solos allows her to be 'heard'. Metaphorically as well as literally she uses her own voice: 'It makes me show that I have a talent – my own, unique talent, my own voice, that's different from other people.'

Sam explained to me that staff had helped her learn to take difficult passages home to look at calmly: 'The music is quite difficult. When you first get it, obviously it's going to be difficult.

So I just focus on it, and I think, if I can't do this bit, take it home, come back, see where else I struggle and just do it in that kind of way.' She would remember tricky bits, so that when repertoire came around again she prepared afresh by taking the part away to practise: 'It's helped with school work as well. Especially when you move into the senior phase of school. You find more things difficult, but you remember, I found this music difficult, and I just took it away and looked at it, and I can do the same for this.'

**'Music takes you places' (i)**

So much for the external processes of learning to make music, but what role does music have with its interior, personal, meaning-making aspects, in developing social and emotional skills in young people? Taylor told me of how playing in Big Noise orchestras 'takes her away' from the troubles of everyday life, family etc. No other activity, she says, totally absorbs her in this way. Sam explained: 'Music takes you places. If you have a bad day, play the music and let it take you where you want to go. . . to any of the good times I've had.'

This aspect of escaping, or perhaps transcending, the everyday situation with its anxieties was a recurring theme amongst my interviewees. Sam spelt out a little more of how music-making functions as a means of becoming connected to and perhaps working through our emotions:

'Sometimes if it's an angry piece and I'm angry I think, This is how I'm feeling, how I relate to the music right now. But if it's a romantic piece I have to picture it so I can get into it. . . put it into a movie. And it helps.'

The act of making music, of playing an instrument, actually brings Sam into a visceral realm, where emotions are faced, are felt within the safe bounds of a piece of music, where 'art' functions to put a frame around our lived experience. Sam tells of a further stage:

> But if there's not an angry piece involved and I'm needing that kind of concentration, then I just take a deep breath in and out and play. And then as soon as I play all my [negative] emotions go away. I feel calm and ready for the next step ahead. Because I know that everything will be ok. As soon as I start playing I know that all these things will go away and that the music will take me somewhere I want to go.

For Amy, the boundaries of the orchestral rehearsal also provide a discipline which she finds liberating:

> Music relaxes me. Playing music – you're sitting there. You can't talk or scream or make noises, you can't fidget, and that's what I used to do. I used to bite my nails. And scratch my knees, but I always knew that if I was sitting there with my instrument I can't fidget, I can't scream or start greeting [crying]. And it would always give me that time to think about stuff.

Amy makes an interesting observation: 'Because it's not pop music, I'm not sitting with the lyrics going round my head. With classical [instrumental] music you're listening to the actual music. It's quite relaxing.' So the abstract quality of the music on its own, without words and their immediacy of meaning to focus thoughts, makes for a relaxing of the mind, the emotions, the spirit, perhaps.

**'Music takes you places' (ii)**

But there is another way that music-making takes these young musicians places. Some of the most formative experiences which the young musicians talked about centred around opportunities for high profile performances or for foreign travel afforded by Big Noise. For example, on 21st June 2012 the young people of Big Noise, Raploch played side-by-side with the members of the Simón Bolìvar Symphony Orchestra of Venezuela, conducted by Gustavo Dudamel. It was an outdoor performance in Raploch in front of 7-8,000 people, broadcast on live national and international television, to mark the opening of the Cultural Olympiad. Joe told me about the build-up to the concert, and the months of hard work in preparation:

> I remember when we first got told about it, we were
> all really excited. We went in to play the pieces for the
> concert, and for the months we were practising we
> thought it was really hard. . . it was too hard, and we
> all got worked really hard too. We all thought
> negative things about that then, but when it came to
> the weeks beforehand, and when the concert came, it
> was really good – really positive.

The Big Concert was an enormous undertaking for Big Noise, in its infancy still, and required a great deal of everyone involved. Yet the experience of reaching the point at which the young people in Raploch could perform at the level they did has proved to be extremely fruitful in terms of motivating the young musicians and fostering a new confidence.

Charlie described what it was like to sit amongst the Venez-uelan players:

> It helps you (sitting side by side) because they've
> done it so many more times, you can kind of follow

> them, follow their body language in a way. It's also
> how they play – how they express when they're
> playing. . . I remember our sound wasn't as good. . .
> but we'd only been playing the pieces for a few
> months. It was going to be really easy for them, and
> that made it easier for them to show off a wee bit. . .
> and sometimes in the concert they really pushed us
> to the same. . . to show off that confidence that they
> had. I remember seeing pictures of them trying to
> push some of the less confident people. With their
> gestures, not words.

The Venezuelan players' tacit acts of nurturing were extra-ordinary to watch; the more experienced musicians leant towards their younger desk partners, and somehow encouraged them to play at a different level. Those of us attending the rehearsals for the Big Concert in 2012 heard the young Raploch musicians' sounds becoming bigger and richer and saw them begin to play in a way they had never done before, as they matched and played inside the sound of their Venezuelan partners.

Amy remembered:

> It was amazing. . . We sound great with these people.
> Just put us with these people all the time! When
> there's a professional sitting beside you and they turn
> round and say, 'Well done! You played that right!' And
> you think, 'I'm good at that. It's not just my teacher
> saying that. . .' I think that all of us, after we played
> with them, we got that confidence boost that we can
> actually do this. If we put our minds to it and played
> this music we could actually end up really good at
> this. I think it gave the whole of Big Noise a kick.

In January 2014 sixty young people from Big Noise, Raploch were invited to Caracas for a week to play side-by-side with musicians from one of the local *nucleos*, culminating in a huge concert. This proved to be a highly motivating experience for the Scottish musicians. Amy remembered with a smile:

> After Venezuela we all came back wanting longer hours and more symphony orchestra. We wanted more discipline. We were playing with this orchestra who were the same age as us. We could see they were better than us. We were sitting there thinking, nope, we're going to be better than you. We're coming back!

The Big Trip to Caracas had left the Raploch young musicians with a sense of confidence to take other challenges and opportunities in their stride, and it had also brought a change of wider perspective. Johnathon explained: 'You see the poverty – the shacks on the side of the hills. It was a real eye opener. It made everyone see how fortunate they are.'

For Johnathon, going to Gothenburg, Sweden with a group from Big Noise Raploch was also a significant time. He played percussion in an orchestra there of mixed ages, from 5 to 17 years old, when he was 15, with many young people coming from the surrounding Nordic countries. Johnathon reflected on what he perceived as: 'A sense of togetherness even though we couldn't communicate. There's something that we can come together and share.'

**Relationships with staff: transforming lives, changing trajectories**

The initial evaluation of Big Noise programmes published in 2015 by the Glasgow Centre for Population Health states:

> A recurring theme. . . is Sistema Scotland's emphasis on the quality of the relationship between musician and participant. . . Indeed many of the strengths of

> Big Noise programme delivery are designed to enable
> opportunities for this relationship to flourish. Sistema
> Scotland's vision could be described as 'people
> change lives' not services or programmes nor music.

Many of the perspectives I gathered from the members of Big Noise Raploch bore out this conclusion. Taylor feels that Big Noise staff have 'been there throughout', listening, making time for her, encouraging her. This seems to have been a major factor in developing the confidence she now has to follow the various courses of study at college necessary for her to follow her dream of becoming a social worker. Without Big Noise, she says she would be out drinking with her friends. As it is, she's always too tired to join them, after taking part in Big Noise! Our conversation leaves me with a strong sense of her determination to complete the study necessary for her to achieve the position in the workplace she desires. Moreover she articulates her vision for what contribution she wants to make to society, in terms of seeing a transformation in how children in care are looked after.

The stability of contact with Big Noise staff members was a recurring theme in our conversations. Many of those mentioned as having played a particular role in young people's lives have been there since the beginning of the programme nine years ago. Another recurring theme was that Big Noise staff treated the young musicians very differently from teachers at school. Their roles were distinct, as their secondary school teachers were focused on learning outcomes, on them achieving well academically, and often had hundreds of young people to deal with each day. In contrast, the 'vibe' is much more 'chilled' at Big Noise, despite the fact that there is pressure, especially leading up to concerts.

Taylor described how much it meant to her that Big Noise staff aren't paid specifically to care for looked-after young people, but instead offer friendship out of a sense of genuinely wanting a relationship with the young musicians. Members of Big Noise staff routinely go out of their way to support the wider needs of the young musicians. For Amy this meant arranging mock interviews so she could gain confidence in readiness for her real interviews to gain training placements in early childcare. For Joe this meant giving him pieces of kit which he needed in order to be able to take up an opportunity to go on an 'eco trip' to Central America, a huge, hard-won and much appreciated opportunity which he delighted in. For every one of the young people I spoke with this meant staff members helping them through difficult stages, quietly coming alongside them, supporting, listening and encouraging them to learn ways of getting through, and giving them resources they could draw upon again and again in their future lives.

Sistema Scotland is funded by a combination of public and private investors including Scottish Government, local authorities and a range of trusts, foundations and individuals who are committed to bringing about permanent social transformation through offering children and young people experiences and opportunities which would not otherwise be open to them. □

# Everyday Courage and Confidence

Heather Zajac

> Heather Zajac worked with the Rock Trust for seven years
> supporting care-experienced young people. The Rock Trust is
> a charity that works with young people between the age of 16
> and 25 who are homeless or at risk of becoming homeless.
> Her role was to support young people through the transition
> from homelessness to finding accommodation and a key part
> of this work was helping to build their resilience. Through her
> work at the Rock Trust, she developed an understanding of the
> complex needs of vulnerable young people. She then went on
> to be the co-ordinator at the Scottish National Social
> Networks, developing projects at a national scale to support
> local authorities to meet the needs of the disadvantaged

I HAVE worked for over twenty years predominantly with young people experiencing homelessness. It astonishes me how resilient they are. Most of the young people I have supported have shown great personal strength and emotional intelligence, but they have limited skills and experience to help them overcome their challenges. One thing they all have in common is hope; no one becomes a young mum believing that her child will be taken into care, and no young person who has lived on the streets and 'sofa surfed' thinks this is a permanent state. They have belief and hope that this time things will work in their favour. Even when they feel everything is against them, they still believe things will improve.

My role has been to support young people through the

transition from homelessness to finding accommodation and a key part of this work is helping to build their resilience. This involves encouraging them to take responsibility, supporting their decisions, helping them over the obstacles and guiding them through the process of becoming more resilient.

Having a youth specific approach is crucial to supporting young people through homelessness. Encouraging young people who often lack confidence, have limited social networks, as well as not having a place they can call home, can have an immense impact on their well-being and motivation. Often the young people feel they are barely surviving and every day feels overwhelming and a challenge. Each time they feel they have grasped the enormity of what's ahead, another issue arises. Unfortunately, things tend to snowball and the problems grow. More issues arise and the challenge just feels too big to address. They feel exhausted, forgotten and helpless. Life is full of ups and downs, but their previous life has not prepared them for this. As a result they find themselves in need of professional support, lacking everyday courage and confidence.

Recently, I facilitated a group work exercise with young people who had faced great challenges in life. My aim was to help them realise their strengths and identify the areas they could develop. All were receiving support from the Rock Trust.

One attendee was an asylum seeker who said he had experienced 18 years of persecution in his home country. He also reported that he sleeps rough on the streets of Edinburgh city centre. He is cold and scared, but still feels safer than he did in his home country. This surprised me. I have supported young people rough sleeping on the streets and I have never felt it was a safe place for anyone to stay. This man also talked about the loss of friends and family back home and how he often feels lonely and isolated. He can go days without speaking to someone or engaging eye contact, but he said his life was no longer in danger and this was the price to pay for feeling safe.

Within the group we recognised and identified each other's strengths and positive qualities, how it was ok to be them. They felt that the motivation to succeed was high. They also felt (especially this young man) that this was not a permanent stage and things would improve. He said that he had sacrificed too much to fail but required support and guidance on how to improve his life.

Another attendee at the group work session described herself as a young carer. She said she had never experienced freedom or had a proper childhood. She gets up every day, helps her mum get out of bed, cooks for all the family, cleans the house, and helps administer medication. She described her daily routine as 'difficult but necessary'. She said she meets everyone's needs and puts her own last (including her education), yet she was full of hope, positivity and, in my opinion, resilience. It was only support from organisations that got her through and provided some respite. Again, she felt low at times, but knew life would not always be so difficult, although she needed reminding of this at times.

What helped her? Positivity and hope? Her mum's condition had stabilised, but she had a progressive illness and her health would not improve. Owing to her engagement with a young carers charity it was identified that support for her mum and a care package needed to be put in place. The school had been informed and updated on the situation and were supporting her to attend and continue her education.

She had expressed an interest in music and, as the Rock Trust had established an ongoing music programme, she attended this on a regular basis. Within the music groups we encouraged participants to express their feelings and hopes. She said this had really helped as she could offload her fears, joys and worries – particularly in writing.

It was during this session that I asked the attendees to describe a resilient person and someone who was not resilient, and then place the descriptive words on a flipchart. As could have been predicted, the two descriptions were very different. Descriptions of a non-resilient person ranged from sad, lonely, low, angry and tired while a resilient person was described as being happy, beautiful and energetic, with lots of friends. When I asked them to describe a person in the limelight that they thought was resilient, they took the view that Britney Spears and Eminem were resilient. The attendees thought that both singers had experienced very public challenges and had overcome them.

What the group came to realise was that resilient people experience times of sadness and despair along with joy and hope. Resilient people are not always energetic and popular. At times they experience all emotions. In order to be resilient you need to reflect, assess and find strength to overcome adversity and face your challenges. If you do this, you can come back stronger. The attendees had all faced challenges and all struggled with some difficulties in their lives.

I tried to convey the message that, to overcome adversity, you need to have coping strategies. It's these strengths that build your resilience. This echoes the old saying, 'What doesn't kill you makes you stronger.' By coping strategies, I meant positive strategies that would help improve the situation: exercise;

talking; bathing; sleep or rest. We need to be kinder to ourselves and respond to our feelings. When we feel overwhelmed, angry, upset or stressed, we need to stop, ask for support, take time out or seek advice. Helping people to describe how they really feel enables them to manage feelings and impulses more successfully in the future. Responding to our feelings has a real impact on how we handle stress.

Most of the young people accessing homeless services had faced terrible challenges and traumas in their lives. Are they being resilient or just surviving? I often see them coping on a day-to-day basis; getting through each hour, fearing the worst and hoping for the best. Are we just seeing the symptoms of deeper entrenched traumas or are they resilient, facing their fears and accepting support when most needed? Many of the homeless young people who request support present with behaviours of poor empathy, self-harm, substance misuse and impulsive, passive/aggressive behaviours. They have limited positive social networks and lack social capital.

For over three years I supported a young woman, Emma, who displayed similar behaviours to many young people who have experienced loss and what felt like rejection at a young age. She had a difficult relationship with her mum. She was placed with foster carers at the age of eight. At twelve her behavioural issues had escalated to the point where she was relocated to a children's residential unit. When she came to the Rock Trust, aged 17, she was homeless and had a criminal record for petty crime. She was angry and dismissive, as well as pleasant and likeable – all behaviours associated with an insecure attachment. This is exactly what the psychologist Mary Ainsworth had observed:

Here children adopt an ambivalent behavioural style towards the attachment figure. The child will commonly exhibit clingy and dependent behaviour but will be rejecting of the attachment figure when they engage in interaction.

The child fails to develop any feelings of security from the attachment figure. Accordingly, they exhibit difficulty moving away from the attachment figure to explore novel surroundings.

I remember meeting Emma for the first time at her temporary accommodation. She had told me that she required help to get more permanent accommodation as she would like to be closer to her mum and build up a relationship. Over the months I supported her, she opened up about her feelings of rejection and loss of the relationship with her mother. She felt her mum favoured her sister who was not placed in care. She did not know who her father was and felt unloved. As a result, she would seek attention from the foster carers, then later the staff at her residential unit. She said she was often in fights, stole from her friends and was angry for most of her childhood. Now she found herself homeless, taking recreational drugs and extremely unhappy. She could see no way forward. Unfortunately her life, was typical of many young women I supported.

Over the years I supported Emma I gained her trust. I also respected her and did not judge her on her past. She gained permanent accommodation nearer her mum, but unfortunately the relationship did not improve. She had a real passion for cooking, enrolling on a cookery programme at her local college. She would often describe the food she had prepared at college and show me pictures on her phone. I asked her why she never took any of the food she had cooked with her? She replied, why would she as she had no one to share and enjoy it with? She had a few friends (most encouraged her to partake in drugs) and was no longer in touch with any family.

After a lot of discussion, we identified a need for a befriender. I co-ordinated a befrienders scheme, recruiting, screening and training volunteers who were willing to give up their time to meet young people on a regular basis. I presented Emma with a range of profiles, providing her with a choice of volunteers with a range of skills. Finally, we arranged a meeting with a befriender which was a big success. They connected right away. Meeting regularly with a volunteer, who was well matched and unpaid, really boosted her confidence. She later told me that all the positive influences in her life were paid staff. To have someone wanting to see her in their own time had a powerful impact on her. At each weekly meeting with the befriender she would bring the food she had prepared and they would enjoy it together. This boosted her confidence, and her skills grew giving her enough confidence to enrol in a full-time course to gain qualifications.

The college she was attending had a Transitions Learning Care (TLC) worker. A key part of this role was to encourage care-experienced people to enrol and start an education. Many had expressed a reluctance to attend further education owing to lack of confidence and prior attainment in education. Another barrier for care-experienced young people was the application form. This requested previous addresses in the last five years. Many care-experienced young people can have multiple placements in temporary accommodation – anything from one home to as many as five or six. In this case Emma was reluctant to put down the name and address of the residential unit in which she had lived. She felt it stigmatised her and would hamper her application. The TLC worker had the authority to override this aspect of the application, keeping these details separate or, in some cases, noting them as 'not relevant'.

Emma attended college for three years, supported by the Rock Trust, her volunteer befriender and the TLC worker. Towards the end of her course an opportunity arose for a placement in a French Patisserie in Paris. Opportunities like that do not come up very often and she was keen to go and learn. Unfortunately, this was a costly trip so I approached the college and explained her circumstances. They agreed to pay half the cost and social services offered a contribution, as did the Rock Trust. However, we still required further funds. A social worker at East Lothian Council heard our plea and offered to sell the produce from her allotment to raise the remaining funds. Emma was over-whelmed by everyone's generosity. This act of kindness had a profound effect on her. She commented that 'never had anyone done anything for me that didn't want something back'. I felt this was a pivotal moment in her life. She attended the place-ment, worked hard and gained her qualification. What's more, she quickly gained full-time employment in a Michelin star restaurant in France! She is a talented chef who now has self-belief and confidence.

We keep in contact. She still has her insecurities but has managed to overcome her feelings of abandonment. She has also met up with her dad and the relationship has been thriving and positive. She still faces challenges, but now has the resilience to overcome them.

Emma had consistent support for four years (and beyond) from volunteers and professionals who cared for her. They were a positive influence, identified her struggles and responded to them. There were clear boundaries and roles. By working in partnership, I feel we overcame the barriers that can prevent professionals from 'putting care into practice' and managed to provide 'corporate parenting', genuinely caring for a young person.

**Future learning**

I now design and deliver training to social care professionals on resilience. This includes how to identify it and support people in recognising their vulnerabilities and strengths. Every time I ask the attendees: What is resilience? the main response are the words 'bounce back'. I used to challenge this and say that 'no one wishes to go back; maybe it's more a case of moving forward'. But when I relate this to events and setbacks within my personal life, I now see that 'bounce back' is a more suitable term. It's bouncing back to your stable place. Getting back up on your feet, and then moving forward. It's bouncing back up, dusting yourself down and then moving in the direction you choose. That's how I now see resilience.

Brigid Daniel, Professor of Social Work at the University of Stirling, completed research on resilience and young people. Within her study she describes the 'Building Blocks of Resilience' and highlights the importance of having a secure base, with a sense of security and attachment. Many of the young people who access homeless services believe they have no secure base and no one to care for or support them through the emotional turmoil of having no home, especially if they are care-experienced. What drives them on to succeed, secure a home and build new relationships?

Daniel's research indicates that if individuals have self-efficacy and a problem-solving attitude it supports them to face their challenges. She states:

> By engaging with children in a way that involves them in assessment and planning, that encourages them to contribute to decisions about their lives and that provides them with positive choices, practitioners could help to create the conditions for the development of better self-efficacy.

I believe empowering young people to be involved in planning and decision-making builds up their resilience. Encouraging dreams, aspirations and the young person's wishes should be at the heart of the plans.

I believe in a coordinated support service. Most people have multiple complex needs and by working collaboratively and sharing learning the people who are supporting them can co-produce services which are helpful and effective.

When I reflect on my own resilience I see myself as a strong, positive, resilient woman. As with most people, I have experienced loss and trauma in my life. What has been especially challenging is facing these setbacks while supporting young people through theirs. As a professional working in this area I am not afraid to say that I have been affected by the lives of the people I have supported. I have sometimes been so concerned for their well-being that I have had sleepless nights. I have unfortunately experienced the loss of the young people I have tried to help. Some have felt overwhelmed by the challenges and felt they can no longer face life. They have tragically been lost to drugs, alcohol and overdose. My colleagues, friends and family have supported me though these difficult days. I also know the loss and grief is permanent, but you learn to deal with them. They become part of you, and eventually happy memories help to balance the loss.

Life can often be full of enormous challenges, past traumas and difficult days, but there is also joy along the journey. No one is completely resilient, we are all vulnerable at times; even superheroes have their weaknesses. It's what makes us human. ☐

# Community Approaches to Growing Resilience

Daniel & Charis Robertson, Hot Chocolate Trust

Charis Robertson is the Assistant Director of Hot Chocolate Trust, an innovative grassroots youth work organisation in Dundee. Hot Chocolate is also part of the movement in Scotland to address Adverse Childhood Experiences (ACEs), deepening their understanding of trauma. Charis explains how the charity has grown over 17 years by building trust with local marginalised young people. Despite their stories of traumatic experiences, shared in this chapter, they proved they could be incredibly intelligent, articulate, creative and a lot of fun. She is clear that Hot Chocolate's experience over the past 17 years demonstrates that poor outcomes in the future are not inevitable. Recovery is possible.

DANIEL (not his real name) is one of the young people who frequently attended the Steeple Church in Dundee where Hot Chocolate Trust offers support for young people.

**Daniel's story**

'Back then we were like a pack of wolves. We'd split up, circle our victim, intimidate them at first and then batter them. We weren't officially a gang, but we basically were. We got a thrill, we got a kick out of it. It was the adrenaline rush from fighting – it felt really good. It was a way to unload all our problems, all our anger onto someone else.

'So when we started coming to Hot Chocolate Trust, we caused a lot of trouble. I remember getting into loads of arguments with the team, and sometimes even violence too. We got banned 13 times in a row – that's a record! Other places would have given up after the first one or two or three. But you guys obviously saw something better in us and thought: we're not gonna give up on these young people. They've had enough people giving up on them. We're not going to play a part in that. And you kept going and kept going and kept going.

'When one of our gang took his own life, I can't describe how I felt. I was torn apart. I turned my house upside down. He was always the quieter one, the sensible one – and I'd just seen him a couple of days before. I just couldn't believe it. But the part that you guys played through that time was massive. That's when we saw that you guys were as upset as us because you'd got to know this great young person, this great character, this loveable guy. Even though you had so much pain and hurt, you still went out your way to open up and make us feel better, to support us, to organise transport for us to get to the funeral. Not many places would do that. That was a big turning point in all our guys' lives.

'But even after all that, one night when I was really drunk, a couple of us broke into the business of a team member's family and stole a bunch of stuff. I find this really hard to talk about actually. In fact, I can't even describe how I feel about it. Every time I saw her afterwards I felt horrible, that I'd let her down. I felt so much shame inside about what I'd done. She handled things really professionally, but I could see she was really upset and disappointed. Even now, years later, I can't believe that she's actually forgiven me.

'When I think about the guy I was back then, I feel totally disgusted with myself. I think about the pain I inflicted – not just physically, but emotionally too. I stopped people from becoming who they should be. I

think a lot about the 'what ifs' in life. I think about what if Hot Chocolate wasn't here? Would I still be doing all those stupid things? Would I be in prison?
I definitely would.

'You went way beyond what you needed to do for me. You visited me in hospital. You took me to court. You let me do my community service with you. You asked me to give the speech on our open night. You gave me a push when I needed it. I'd come in and you'd say, what's wrong? – you just knew when something was wrong. You gave me the love and boundaries that I needed. You gave me a home and family. You taught me how to be a respectable young man.

'There's a lot of joy and good memories in my story – but there's a lot that's upsetting too. I don't mind speaking about it though – in fact I'd rather speak about it than keep it to myself. I want to spread my stories and the things I've done and what I've learnt.
I want people to know that they're not the only ones dealing with these problems.

'I used to be the guy who caused trouble and picked fights, now I'm the person who stops others from doing that – I go out of my way to make sure other young people are safe. Without you guys I don't know where any of us would have been. Most of us have got kids, partners and are doing well. I'm surprised I am where I am right now. I have a home, a family, a puppy. I have a front and back garden! Sometimes I wake up and think, how did I get here? Why did I wait this long to get here?' – Daniel

## Background

Hot Chocolate Trust is a grassroots youth work organisation based in the centre of Dundee. We began in 2001 when a part time youth worker and a small team of volunteers ventured out from the Steeple Church to try to connect with the scores of young people who were hanging out on the grass just outside the church. Because of the dreich Scottish weather, the team took some hot chocolate out as a way to break the ice (hence our name!). There was no defined agenda, other than to try and get to know these young people and hear their stories and see if something might emerge from those interactions.

Over time and as trust was built, the young people started sharing their stories. They proved to be incredibly intelligent, articulate, creative and a lot of fun. They shared insights into their 'alternative' subculture, offering thoughtful and challenging reflections on how their piercings, tattoos, brightly coloured hair, metal music, skateboarding, and graffiti art expressed their sense of identity. They also spoke about the tough realities of their lives, with recurring themes of truancy and school exclusion, homelessness, unemployment, substance misuse, encounters with the criminal justice system, traumatic experiences, and a sense of marginalisation from their local communities, schools, and often even families. They hung out in town because they didn't feel they belonged anywhere else in the city. They hung out with other 'misfits' because that's when they felt they could be themselves. They had developed their own ways of being which helped them grow more resilient.

Recognising the deep need in the young people for a sense of belonging, the team asked the young people what they might do if they had some space inside the church building. Soon after, they started using the sanctuary space to rehearse with their thrash metal bands and using the vestry phone and computer to help with making appointments, writing CVs and the like.

Seventeen years later, Hot Chocolate is an independent charity and has expanded substantially. And although we are still housed in the church, we now have lots of dedicated space: an art room, a music room, a sports hall, a chilling room, a quiet room, and office space to house the 12 staff and 20+ volunteers who work with us from month to month. We work with around 300 young people each year, through drop-ins, individual support, group work, creative projects and residential weekends. The young people grow to feel a deep sense of ownership of, pride in, and responsibility for the place. . . although of course that is not necessarily an easy process and can take some time and a great deal of energy – as seen in Daniel's story! But as a result of this approach, we have never needed to advertise the work of Hot Chocolate: the young people come because their friends have told them it's a good place to be.

Our scale may have changed since those early days, but our core ethos remains. Our work is relational, holistic and long term. We always start with the assumption that the young people have talents and skills and strengths, and we seek to nurture these. We are careful about our language: we are not a service *for* the young people but are growing a community *with* them. Team members are quick to encourage young people to take up responsibility for the community, whether giving guests or funders a tour of the space, decorating rooms, developing new projects, recruiting new staff members, being trusted with keys to the building, shaping our strategic plans or, indeed co-writing a book chapter together. We strongly believe that the young people are experts of their own experiences, and therefore we must learn from them. In our experience, collaboration and genuine reciprocal relationships are where the life transforming magic happens. And when we consider the realities that many

129

of the young people are facing, it is not difficult to see why nurturing resilience really matters.

## Adverse Childhood Experiences

There has been a growing movement in Scotland around adverse childhood experiences (ACEs) and trauma in the past couple of years. (Carol Craig's excellent book *Hiding In Plain Sight*, 2017 is well worth a read for a fuller exploration into ACEs.) Hot Chocolate has been part of that movement, deliberately deepening our understanding of trauma, undertaking research with our young people around their experiences of it, and implementing plans to develop trauma-informed practice across our team.

This national ACEs interest is based on a large scale research study undertaken in the States between 1995-97, where public health doctors asked participants to score themselves against ten key indicators of adversity in childhood (under the headings of abuse, neglect and household challenges), and compared this with their health and well-being outcomes in adulthood. The conclusions were startling: people scoring 4+ of the ten ACE indicators were significantly more likely to develop harmful behaviours including smoking, harmful alcohol use, drug use, risky sexual behaviour, violence and crime – and are also linked to diseases such as diabetes, cancer and cardiovascular disease.

The same research questions were used in 2015 by Public Health Wales NHS Trust, who found that 14 per cent of the Welsh population scored 4 or higher. Hot Chocolate also used these questions in 2017 as part of our annual confidential community 'census'. A sobering 56 per cent of the young people scored 4+, and tragically 24 per cent scored 7+. What we had known anecdotally since our earliest days was suddenly confirmed with some pretty stark statistics.

However, thankfully, what is also known from the research, as well as from our own experience over the past 17 years is that poor outcomes in the future are *not* inevitable. Recovery is possible. There is hope!

**Daniel**

Let's revisit Daniel's story: a young man who had suffered a huge amount of adversity in his childhood and adolescence, whose destructive behaviours were clearly an out-working of that pain. But his reflections and analysis on what helped him to heal and move on with his life are fascinating and incredibly important for us to hear, and can be broken down into three key themes:

1) Hot Chocolate was the 'opposite of trauma'.

> 'You saw something better in us.'

> 'You thought: We're not going to give up on these young people.

> 'You gave me love and boundaries.'

If trauma is something that is unpredictable, scary, negative and is done *to* you, Hot Chocolate worked hard to be the opposite of that for Daniel and his peers. We tried as hard as possible to provide a safe space which was clear in terms of expectations and boundaries within our community – and brought challenge to the group if these boundaries were overstepped. As a result, we were a predictable and consistent presence, offering an important relief from some of the chaos and confusion in other parts of their lives. When the team did have to 'bring challenge' (normally asking them to leave due to threatening or violent behaviours towards others), this was always framed with regret, with love, with the promise of second chances (and third and fourth ones), and with affirmations about the skills, talents and potential we saw in them. This was especially important, to not feed into the group's negative sense of self-worth.

2) Relationships

> 'Even though you had a lot of pain and hurt.'

> 'You went out of your way.'

> 'She's actually forgiven me.'

> 'You just knew when something was wrong.'

> 'You gave me a home and a family.'

As Daniel stated, the turning point was when he and the group saw how upset the Hot Chocolate team were by the death of one of their friends. Whilst our focus was firmly on supporting the community of hurting and vulnerable young people through their shock and grief, we were also not afraid to show our own emotion. For young people whose main experience of adults was either disappointment or suspicion around their motives, it was through this terrible time that they came to realise that the Hot Chocolate team really did care for them and that adults could be trusted. Following this tragedy, Daniel and the group began letting their guard down with us, and over the next couple of years became the fiercest champions and advocates of Hot Chocolate imaginable!

3) Using their voice

> 'I'd rather speak about it than keep it to myself'

Hot Chocolate does not view the young people we work with as victims. They are survivors. They are resilient. They are dreamers about a better future. They want their experiences to count for something. And they want to make a difference in the world. Over the past four years, we have developed an ethical life-storytelling methodology, enabling young people (past and present) to share their stories safely, to make sense of their experiences, to process some of the pain and trauma from their lives, to look towards a better future. The honesty, vulnerability and impact of these stories is only possible due to the long term trusting relationships that exists between the story-tellers and the Hot Chocolate team. Most who have been involved with this life-storytelling process (like Daniel) have chosen to also have their stories anonymously recorded to be shared with other young people, professionals and policy makers. As a result, these story-tellers have expressed a significant sense of healing, empowerment and hope for the future. And increasingly Hot Chocolate sees a key part of our responsibility (and frankly, privilege) as being able to help amplify the voices of the young people, so that people in power might sit up and pay attention to these incredible young people.

**A wider resilience agenda**

The Public Health Wales NHS Trust have now published a follow-up study to their original 2015 ACEs project: *Sources of resilience and their moderating relationships with harms from adverse childhood experiences.* One of their main conclusions is as follows:

> Childhood [0-18 years] resilience moderates the
> increased risks to mental health from ACEs. Personal,
> relationship and community resilience resources such

as social and emotional skills, childhood role models, peer support, connections with school, understanding how to access community support, and a sense that your community is fair to you are strongly linked to reduced risks of mental illness across the life course. High childhood resilience is related to substantial reductions in lifetime mental illness and potentially offers protections even in those with no ACEs. . .

Such a strong emphasis on the role of community from this study is welcomed (particularly the importance of relationships and the sense that your community is fair to you), and resonates with both the experience of Hot Chocolate over the past 17 years and also with Daniel's own story.

Too often resilience is framed as an individual's own responsibility: 'if only they tried harder. . .', 'if only they turned up for their appointment. . .', 'if only they stopped taking drugs. . .' This is at best naive, and at worst dangerous, placing blame on individuals without recognising the surrounding socio-, economic and political complexities, of which we are all a part.

It is also not good enough to pursue a resilience agenda in order to help people simply cope with their adverse situations, without also tackling the unjust powers, systems and structures which lie at the root of many of the ACEs experienced by our young people. For only then will we see the cycles broken and reduced negative outcomes in future generations. Hot Chocolate holds a more radical perspective towards resilience, seeking to stir up a critical awareness and activism amongst our community. By amplifying the voices of the young people in our community, and encouraging decision makers and politicians to act on what these voices say, we seek to to ensure more people get the front and back garden that they've always dreamt of.  □

# References

This is a list of key references for each chapter.
A list of references, with live links, is available online.
Go to: www.postcardsfromscotland/book15.html

**Building Resilience through Support and Challenge: The Golden Mean in Action** Alan McLean

McLEAN, A., 2003. *The Motivated School.* London: Sage

McLEAN, A., 2009. *Motivating Every Learner* London: Sage

McLEAN, A., 2017. *Knowing and Growing: Insights for Developing Ourselves and Others.* Paisley: CCWB Press

For access to Alan Mclean's free online profiles go to: www.whatmotivateslearning.com

**From One Extreme to Another: Parenting in Scotland**
Carol Craig

CRAIG, C., 2018. 'Scotland the Cruel: The legacy of our sadistic past' *Scottish Review,* March 2018

CRAIG, C., 2017. *Hiding in Plain Sight.* Paisley: CCWB Press

CRAIG, C., 2007. *Creating Confidence: A Handbook for Professionals Working with Young People.* Paisley: CCWB Press

GUNDERSON, E. A., GRIPSHOVER, S. J., ROMERO, C., DWECK, C.S., GOLDIN-MEADOW, S., LEVINE, S., 2013. 'Parent Praise Predicts Children's Motivational Frameworks Five Years Later' *Child Development*, February 2013, vol. 85, no. 5

MACCOBY, E.E., MARTIN, J.A., 1983 'Socialization in the context of the family: Parent-child interaction'. In: Hetherington,

E.M., Ed., *Handbook of Child Psychology: (Vol. 4.) Socialization, Personality, and Social Development*, 4th Edition. New York: Routledge

MASUD, H., RAMAYAH, T., SHAKIL, A. M., 2014. 'Parenting styles and academic achievement of young adolescents: A systematic literature review'. *Quality and Quantity*: 49

'Scottish Children Among least active', 2016. BBC online

SHONKOFF, J. P., 2010. 'Building a New Biodevelopment Framework to Guide the Future of Early Childhood Policy'. *Child Development*, February 2010, vol. 81, no. 1

**The Silence of the Weans** Sue Palmer

MANOWALAILAO, R., 2017. *'What is ECCE?' UNESCO: Education for All*

WHITBREAD, D., 2017. 'Free Play and Children's Mental Health'. *The Lancet: Child and Adolescent Health* vol. 1, no. 3

**Learning Outdoors: Healthy Challenges for All**
Chalmers Smith

CHEESMOND, J., 1979. 'Research Review of the Outdoor Education Programme in Lothian Region Secondary Schools 1978/1979 Edinburgh', Edinburgh: Lothian Region and Dunfermline College of Education

FINNISH NATIONAL AGENCY for EDUCATION. 2017. *Finnish education in a nutshell.* Finland: Ministry of Education and Culture

MANNION, G., MATTU, L., WILSON, M., 2015. 'Teaching, learning, and play in the outdoors: a survey of school and pre-school provision in Scotland'. Perth: Scottish Natural Heritage Commissioned Report No. 779

NICOL, R., HIGGINS, P., ROSS, H., MANNION, G., 2007. 'Outdoor education in Scotland: a summary of recent research'. Perth: Scottish Natural Heritage

PRETTY, J., GRIFFIN, M., PEACOCK, J., HINE, R., SELLENS, M., SOUTH, N., 2005. 'A Countryside for Health and Wellbeing: The Physical and Mental Health Benefits of Green Exercise'. Colchester: University of Essex Report for the Countryside Recreation Network

RUBENS, D., 1997. 'Outdoor Education, Adventure and Learning – a Fusion'. MSc (Education) Degree. Edinburgh: University of Edinburgh

**Whitdale Primary School: Resilience and *Bounce Back!***
Iain McDermott

BOXHALL, M., 2002. *Nurture Groups in Schools: Principles and Practice.* London: Chapman

CAIRNS, B., & HARKER, M., 2008. *Empowering Change.* Edinburgh: Scottish Government

NOBLE, T., McGRATH, H., *Bounce Back!*, 2011. Melbourne: Pearson

SELIGMAN, M., 2011. *Flourish.* New York: Simon and Schuster

SELIGMAN, M., PETERSON, C., McGRATH, R., 2001. *Values in Action Survey of Character Strengths*. VIA Institute on Character

**Transforming Trajectories: Confidence and resilience-building in the Big Noise** Kathryn Jourdan

GLASGOW CENTRE FOR POPULATION HEALTH, 2015. 'Evaluating Sistema Scotland – initial findings report', 2015. Glasgow: GCPH

**Everyday Courage and Confidence**  Heather Zajac

AINSWORTH, M., 1969. 'Object Relations, Dependency and Attachment: A Theoretical Review of the Infant-Mother Relationship'. *Child Development*, December 1969, vol., 40, no. 4

DANIEL, B., VINCENT, S., FARRALL, E., ARNEY, F., 2009. 'How is the Concept of Resilience Operationalised in Practice with Vulnerable Children?' *International Journal of Child & Family Welfare*. 12


**Community Approaches to Building Resilience**  Daniel and Charis Robertson

BELLIS, M. A., ASHTON, K., HUGHES, K., FORD, K., BISHOP, J., PARANJOTHY, S., 2015. *Adverse Childhood Experiences and their impact on health-harming behaviours in the Welsh adult population.* Cardiff: Public Health Wales NHS Trust

CRAIG, C., 2017. *Hiding in Plain Sight.* Paisley: CCWB Press

HUGHES, K., FORD, K., DAVIES, A.R., HOMOLOVA, L., BELLIS, M.A., 2018.  *Sources of resilience and their moderating relationships with harms from adverse childhood experiences.* Cardiff: Public Health Wales NHS Trust

# Acknowledgements

**Morag Kerr: Editor**
I would like to thank all the authors who have contributed to this book for the time and effort they have put into creating their inspirational accounts of what helps to build resilience and confidence. Alan McLean and Carol Craig have been my mentors over many years and I thank them for sharing their wisdom and knowledge. A special thank you to Carol for giving me the opportunity to work with the wonderful people who wrote this book.

**From One Extreme to Another – Parenting in Scotland: Carol Craig**
Thanks to Suzanne Zeedyk for taking the time to have an extended conversation about my chapter. Thanks are also due to Juliet Hancock for her comments. I also greatly appreciate the discussions I have had over the years with countless teachers, headteachers and parents.

**Learning Outdoors: Chalmers Smith**
I wish to thank Juliet Robertson of the Creative Star Learning Limited and Professor Peter Higgins of the University of Edinburgh for their contributions to, and suggestions for, this chapter and for their assistance, guidance and unbridled enthusiasm for learning outdoors.

**The View from Room 13: Claire Newman**
Thank you to the six people who consented to interview as I researched this piece: William Landsborough, Ruaridh MacInnes, Ciara McCartney, Karen Russell, Sheila Ann Ryan and Sammy Stuart White. Although only half of those I interviewed found their way into the final text, I am grateful to all for their words and wisdom; each conversation proved influential to the writing of the piece. I would also like to thank Rob Fairley, Mark Graham, David Lamont, Sebastian MacMillan, Rebecca MacDougall, Richard Bracken and Sarah Hughes.

**Whitdale Primary School – Resilience and *Bounce Back!*: Iain McDermott**

I would like to thank all of the staff, pupils and parents at Whitdale Primary for their commitment and enthusiasm for creating such a wonderfully resilient school community and the West Lothian Educational Psychology service for the ongoing passion for and drive to ensuring partnership with schools across the county.

**Everyday Courage and Confidence: Heather Zajac**

I would like to thank East Lothian council and the Rock Trust for the opportunities and experience. Also to the young people especially 'the lass from the Riff Raff Crew' – she will know who she is.

## Other books in the series

**1. AfterNow –** What next for a healthy Scotland?
| *Phil Hanlon/Sandra Carlisle*
The authors of this visionary book look at health in Scotland and
beyond health to the main social, economic, environmental and
cultural challenges of our times. They examine the type of
transformational change required to create a more resilient and
healthy Scotland.

**2. The Great Takeover** – How materialism, the media and
markets now dominate our lives | *Carol Craig*
Describes the dominance of materalist values, the media and
business in all our lives and how this is leading to a loss of
individual and collective well-being. It looks at many of the big
issues of our times – debt, inequality, political apathy, loss of self-
esteem, pornography and the rise of celebrity culture. The
conclusion is simple and ultimately hopeful – we can change our
values and our lives.

**3. The New Road** – Charting Scotland's inspirational
communities | *Alf Young / Ewan Young*
A father and son go on a week long journey round Scotland to
see at first hand some of the great environmental, social,
employment and regeneration projects which are happening.
From Dunbar in the south east of Scotland to Knoydart in the
north west they meet people involved in projects which
demonstrate new ways of living.

### 4. Scotland's Local Food Revolution | *Mike Small*

Lifts the lid on the unsavoury reality of our current food system including horsemeat in processed beef products, the unsustainable movement of food round the globe, and how supermarket shopping generates massive waste. It's an indictment of a food syste that is out of control. But there is hope – the growth and strength of Scotland's local food movement.

### 5. Letting Go – Breathing new life into organisations | *Tony Miller/ Gordon Hall*

It is now commonplace for employees to feel frustrated at work – ground down by systems that are dominated by rules, protocols, guidelines, targets and inspections. Tony Miller and Gordon Hall explore the origins of 'command and control' management as well as the tyranny of modern day 'performance management'. Effective leaders, they argue, should 'let go' of their ideas on controlling staff and nurture intrinsic motivation instead.

### 6. Raising Spirits – Allotments, well-being and community | *Jenny Mollison/ Judy Wilkinson/ Rona Wilkinson*

Allotments are the unsung story of our times; hidden places for food, friendship and freedom from the conformity of everyday life. A fascinating look at how allotments came about; why they can make such a substantial contribution to health, well-being, community, food production, and the environment; and what's happening in other countries.

### 7. Schooling Scotland – Education, equity and community | *Daniel Murphy*

The Scottish schooling system does well for many children growing up in Scotland, but to ensure that all children get the education they deserve, a better partnership of parent, child, school, government and society is needed – one to which all Scotland can contribute and from which all children can benefit. Daniel Murphy suggests eight ways to ensure that Scottish education could be stronger and fairer.

### 8. Shaping our Global Future – A guide for young people | *Derek Brown*

Young people worry about the future world they will live in: personal futures, families and jobs. But they also worry about their global futures. The possibilities and challenges ahead appear overwhelming. This guide to human achievements and future challenges is designed to help young people consider the future their children and grandchildren will inhabit.

**9. Conviction** – Violence, culture and a shared public service agenda | *John Carnochan* Policeman John Carnochan takes us on a memorable journey of discovery as he comes to grips with violence and Scotland's traditionally high murder rate. He also gives a fascinating insight into the work of Scotland's Violence Reduction Unit and why it has been so spectacularly successful. This compelling book is not about high visibility policing or more officers but the importance of empathy and children's early years.

**10. She, He, They** – Families, gender and coping with transition | *Shirley Young*
How challenging can gender transition be for both parents and siblings? A story of hope and resilience, it shows that if parents can move beyond the shock and pain of their offspring's transition, all family members can come closer together and experience life-enhancing change.

**11. Knowing and Growing** – Insights for developing ourselves and others | *Alan McLean*
This extraordinary book provides insights and practical tools to help you navigate everyday human interactions, balance your own and others' needs and utilise your emotions to create a more fulfilling life. The powerful insights readers glean from 'McLean's Ring' are not only helpful for parents, teachers and leaders they are also essential for anyone aiming to encourage others to grow and develop as individuals.

**12. Working for Equality** – Policy, politics people |
*Richard Freeman, Fiona McHardy, Danny Murphy* (Editors)
Brings together 22 experienced practitioners from across the country to reflect on equality/inequality – in class, race, gender, poverty, disability and homelessness as well as health and education. They are concerned about individuals as well as ideas and policy instruments. Short and accessible, a pause for thought and inspiration for those concerned with action.

**13. Hiding in Plain Sight** – Exploring Scotland's ill health | *Carol Craig* Scotland. A country that prides itself on its modernity and progressive instincts. Yet this is a nation whose mental and physical health outcomes are poor by European standards. This book asks why? Grippingly readable yet challenging, Carol Craig offers an answer which is glaringly obvious. Generations of Scottish children have suffered in ways that undermine the nation's health. Starting from her own and her neighbours' lives, she explores the growing awareness internationally of the impact of Adverse Childhood Experiences.

**14. Right from the Start** – Investing in parents and babies | *Alan Sinclair* Scotland languishes in the second division of global child well-being. One child in every four is judged to be 'vulnerable' when they enter primary school. Alan Sinclair reveals the harm inflicted on so many of our youngest, most defenceless citizens through a toxic mix of poor parenting, bad health and a society focussed on dealing with consequences rather than causes. He also sets out a routemap for us to start putting children first by helping us all to become better parents.

More titles are planned for 2019.
Books can be ordered from www.postcardsfromscotland.co.uk or from www.amazon.co.uk Kindle editions are also available for some titles.